The Magical CTE Classroom is a refreshing take on how we approach teaching and learning in career and technical education. There are so many lessons to learn and so many ways to incorporate aspects of play and joy into our CTE curriculum. Tisha Richmond has laid out a masterful, playful, easy way to open up learners' minds everywhere! Her approach is relatable, vulnerable, and filled with practical applications that educators can bring to life immediately.

—**Rachael Mann,** speaker, author, consultant

PRAISE FOR *THE MAGICAL CTE CLASSROOM*

In *The Magical CTE Classroom*, Tisha Richmond reminds us that joy isn't just a bonus in education, it's the foundation. Through her powerful storytelling and practical strategies, she helps educators design learning that sparks curiosity, connection, and confidence. With countless ready-to-implement ideas and inclusive activities, this book shows that "routine doesn't mean boring" and that taking risks in the classroom can look like both reinvention and restraint. Tisha's wisdom will leave you inspired to transform your classroom into a place where students don't just show up, they light up.

—**Annick Rauch,** grade 1 French immersion teacher, learner, mom

Tisha has done it again with an inspiring book! Each chapter is filled with real, raw stories and engaging strategies. She includes examples and variations that can be easily implemented and adapted for all educators, especially FCS and other CTE teachers. She offers practical ideas for remixing games, creating learning experiences, and implementing reflection opportunities that are interactive, meaningful, and fun. Her sense of humor, passion, and joy shine through every page! Tisha's work reminds us that when we teach with joy, we create magic that students never forget.

—**Miranda Bright,** human sciences and education career field specialist

This book helped me reset my mindset, redefine my attitude, and bring life back into my classroom. It reminded me why I chose to teach family and consumer sciences in the first place. The pages are packed with inspiration—stories that encouraged me, practical ideas I could implement immediately, and endless possibilities to elevate my students' CTE experience through hands-on learning, creativity, play, and real-world application. *Make Learning Magical* sparked my teaching style, now *The Magical CTE Classroom: Bringing Play, Innovation, and Joy into CTE* expands and deepens it—giving me new ways to innovate, connect, and bring joy back into teaching.

—**Alaina Tharp,** family and consumer science teacher, Ohio

Magic in education doesn't happen by accident, it happens by design, and Tisha Richmond has written the blueprint. *The Magical CTE Classroom* invites educators to teach with more imagination, intention, and joy—because every student deserves learning that feels meaningful, inspiring, and full of possibility. Tisha proves that play isn't a detour from learning, but a direct path to relevance, connection, and lasting impact. This book will change how you see what's possible when courage, creativity, and curiosity lead the way. It's not just a book CTE teachers will love, it's one our classrooms have been waiting for.

—**Elisabeth Bostwick,** author of *Take the L.E.A.P.: Ignite a Culture of Innovation*, speaker, and marketing manager at Brisk Teaching

In this book Tisha Richmond provides support and strategies to CTE teachers about how to create magic and joy in their classrooms. Her narrative is anchored in both research and experience in a culinary classroom. Even though I am not a CTE teacher, I feel like the big ideas, activities, and strategies presented here could be applied to any classroom and in any grade. Thoughtful, practical, and full of creative and innovative ideas, The *Magical CTE Classroom* is a book that any teacher would come back to again and again for inspiration and classroom magic!

—**Jennifer Casa-Todd,** educator, author, keynote speaker

As someone who has dedicated my career to empowering educators and helping them harness innovation for meaningful student impact, I felt both seen and inspired while reading. The author masterfully blends practical lesson ideas with a spirit of joyful learning, offering authentic strategies that spark creativity, connection, and purpose in every classroom.

One of my favorite parts is the thoughtful AI prompts woven throughout the book; they empower educators to plan more efficiently and imagine more boldly. This book uplifts the everyday teacher, the dreamer, the doer, the believer in every students' potential, and reminds us why we teach. It's a must-read for anyone seeking to bring more innovation, joy, and heart into their classroom.

—**Jeni Long,** solutions architect, MagicSchool AI

THE MAGICAL CTE CLASSROOM

THE Magical CTE CLASSROOM

Bringing Play, Innovation, and Joy into Career and Technical Education

Tisha Richmond

The Magical CTE Classroom: Bringing Play, Innovation, and Joy into Career and Technical Education
© 2025 Tisha Richmond

All rights reserved. No part of this publication may be reproduced in any form or by any electronic or mechanical means, including information storage and retrieval systems, without permission in writing by the publisher, except by a reviewer who may quote brief passages in a review. For information regarding permission, contact the publisher at books@daveburgessconsulting.com.

> This book is available at special discounts when purchased in quantity for educational purposes or for use as premiums, promotions, or fundraisers. For inquiries and details, contact the publisher at books@daveburgessconsulting.com.

Published by Dave Burgess Consulting, Inc.
Vancouver, WA
DaveBurgessConsulting.com

Paperback ISBN: 978-1-968898-09-0
Ebook ISBN: 978-1-968898-10-6

Cover and interior design by Liz Schreiter
Edited and produced by Reading List Editorial
ReadingListEditorial.com

Russ, Ella, and Tommy,

You have always brought endless laughter, joy, and heart to every day. Whether playing games or cheering through a reality game show finale, you remind me that the real magic is found in the memories we create and the joy we bring each other.

Contents

Introduction: Returning to the Classroom . . . Is Learning Still Magical? 1

Chapter 1: Have Fun. Be Fearless. 4

Chapter 2: Building the Framework for Joyful Learning 10

Chapter 3: Where the Magic Begins 27

   Community First: The Magical Mystery Relationship-Building Tour 31

      Magical Mystery Classroom Tour 32

   More Activities for Building Community, One Challenge at a Time 35

      Say My Name 35

      Two Truths and a Fib 36

      Marshmallow Challenge 37

      Silent LEGO Build 39

      Back-to-Back LEGO Challenge 40

      Mystery Puzzle 41

      Tumbling Towers 42

      Play-Doh Magic 43

   From Community to Curiosity: The Power of the Hook 44

      "Who Knew?" Hook 45

      Mystery Bag Hook 45

      The Curiosity Box Hook 45

      Flashback Hook 46

      Pixel Reveal Hook 46

      Debatable Hook 46

Chapter 4: Gamified Experiences **48**

Board Game Remix: Fueling Creativity, Collaboration, and
Curiosity in Every Turn. 49
    Name Five 50
    EduScattergories Remix 52
    EduScattergories Categories 53

Words at Play: Reimagining Vocabulary Through Games 55
    Time's Ticking 57
    Top of Mind 58
    Wild Unicorn 60
    EduTaboo 62
    Reverse Charades 63

Playing It Back: Using Games for Reflection and Growth 65
    Operation Skill Game 66
    Kings Corner 68
    Happy Dragon 70

Chapter 5: When Creativity, Curiosity, and Collaboration Collide   **74**

Happy Little Accidents 76
    Squiggle Your Learning 77
    Squiggle Creativity Activity 79

Mystery Missions: Where Curiosity Leads and Creativity Grows ... 87
    Mystery Item Challenge 88
    Mystery Recipe Challenge 89
    Four Pics, One Word 91
    Convince Me 92
    Mind Match 93
    Connect the Blots 94
    Content Connection 95
    Picture This 97

Chapter 6: Lights, Camera, Learn **100**
    The Chopped Challenge 111
    Shark Tank Challenge 113

    Amazing Race Challenge 115
    The Cutthroat Challenge 117
    Crime Scene Kitchen 119
    Mystery Recipe Dash 122

  Classic Game Shows Reimagined for the Classroom 124
    The Price Is Right Hi Lo Challenge 125
    Vocabulary Pyramid Challenge 128
    Skill Showdown 130
    Guess the Term 132

Chapter 7: AI as a Creative Partner for Gamified Learning 136

Chapter 8: Creating an Inclusive and Joyful CTE Classroom ... 148

Chapter 9: From Tears to Triumph 160

Acknowledgments 167
About Tisha Richmond 168
More from Dave Burgess Consulting, Inc. 169

INTRODUCTION

Returning to the Classroom...
Is Learning Still Magical?

Ten years ago, I was a burnt-out, frustrated teacher on the verge of leaving education in search of something more. I never could have imagined that I was about to embark on a journey that would not only reignite my passion but also reveal seven keys to unlocking magical learning in my classroom. These keys didn't just transform education for my students; they transformed me as a teacher. Through play, curiosity, and creativity, I rediscovered the joy I thought I had lost forever. That journey led me to write *Make Learning MAGICAL*, a book that captured my transformation from an exhausted educator to one who embraced teaching with renewed energy and purpose, creating unforgettable experiences in the classroom. But that was just the beginning. For the last six years, I've had the privilege of coaching educators as a tech-integration specialist and consultant, and I've worked as a professional speaker, inspiring others to infuse joy into their teaching, amplifying my impact beyond the walls of my own classroom.

But last fall, something happened that I didn't expect . . .

I found myself pulled back to the very place where my passion for learning was born, the career and technical education (CTE) classroom, teaching culinary arts. It was sudden. It was unexpected. It was exactly where I needed to be. I knew I made the right choice. However,

I was faced with many questions, some of my own and some from others. One that I was asked repeatedly was, "Are kids different now?"

From my perspective? Yes . . . and no.

Students today face more distractions than ever: devices, social media, and the rapid pace of the digital world constantly competing for their attention. Many struggle with executive function skills, focus, and motivation in ways that seem amplified compared to years past. They are navigating a postpandemic educational landscape, carrying experiences that have reshaped their expectations of school. But at the core, kids haven't changed as much as we think. They still crave learning that feels meaningful and relevant, authentic connection, and opportunities to be creative, take risks, and play.

The MAGICAL principles and strategies shared in *Make Learning MAGICAL* hold as true today as ever (don't worry, we'll break down the acronym soon). They are key elements for making learning authentic, relevant, and deeply engaging. In this book, I build on the foundation of *Make Learning MAGICAL* to bring you new ready-to-use strategies, classroom-tested ideas, and fresh approaches to take engagement to the next level and help you bring joyful learning to your classroom.

Each section of this book is designed to help you reignite excitement in your classroom while embracing the evolving needs of today's students. In these pages, you'll find:

* Step-by-step learning experience and unit-planning tools that blend the MAGICAL framework with research-based lesson-planning models.
* Strategies that transform everyday lessons into immersive, gamified experiences.
* Reality TV–inspired challenges that engage students through competition, collaboration, and creativity.
* AI-powered teaching tools to help you generate ideas, create game mechanics, and personalize learning.

- Inclusive strategies to ensure all students, including neurodivergent learners, can thrive.

My hope is that this book will be one that you'll turn to time and time again for ideas, inspiration, and a dose of joy right when you need it. While the world of education continues to evolve, one thing I've found that holds true is that students learn best when they're engaged, curious, and having fun. You hold the key to unlock that magic for your students. Are you ready? Let's begin the adventure!

CHAPTER 1

Have Fun. Be Fearless.

NO RISK, NO MAGIC

"Why did you return to teaching?" This is another question I've been asked repeatedly over the course of this past school year. The truth is, at first, I wasn't really sure. I had a pretty great gig as a learning consultant for an educational company I greatly believe in. I had the flexibility to schedule midday appointments and lunch with friends. I was able to support districts and present to educators around the globe about bringing creativity and collaboration into education. I really did enjoy my work, and it enabled me to grow me in ways that I hadn't experienced before.

When the opportunity to return to the classroom presented itself, it came in the form of another question: "Are you at all curious?" Those who know me know that this was the perfect hook. Curious is my middle name. And so the adventure began.

Though I was comfortable in my consultant role, something was missing. I didn't realize what it was until I was approached with the opportunity to return to the classroom. It was the spark of everyday magic, the messy, unpredictable, beautiful experience of working with students daily.

Stepping back into teaching this past year has felt like jumping into the unknown all over again. I'm not going to lie—my confidence wavered. I wasn't sure if I was the same teacher I had been before, and

I wasn't sure that the classroom was the same either. Life had changed. Education had changed. I had changed.

It would have been easier to stay where I was. However, the greatest lesson I've learned over the past decade is that the most extraordinary moments happen when we take a risk, step out of our comfort zones, and trust that something magical is waiting on the other side of fear. I'm so glad I said yes to shaking things up and entering the world of teaching again.

Has it been easy? Um, no . . . not at all. The past nine months have been a reminder that growth is uncomfortable. I have felt both invigorated and absolutely exhausted. Has it been like riding a bike? Well, yeah—a really rusty one that needs new tires and maybe a comfier seat cushion. Some days, I leave my classroom feeling triumphant and others feeling defeated, wondering, "What in the heck have I done?" But there have been many powerful joyful moments that remind me beyond a shadow of a doubt of the reason why I said yes to teaching: A student who is struggling to stay in school tells me they show up to my class because they love to cook and feel a sense of belonging. A kitchen team that started off the year unsure and collaborating awkwardly is now laughing and creating an incredible dish together. A lesson doesn't go as planned, but the flexibility to refine and pivot leads to a new idea that becomes a go-to strategy. A student from last semester goes out of their way to stop by and invite me to a musical they are performing in. These joyful moments don't happen without risk, stepping into the unknown, embracing the uncertainty, and trusting that even when it feels messy, something magical is cooking.

Returning to the classroom has given me a deeper appreciation and gratitude for teaching. In the midst of the risk, the unknown, and the messy middle, there is an undeniable realization that the work matters a lot. When we realize the profound impact we can make in the lives of children, it centers us and helps us remember our *why* even on the days that are super tough.

And here's what I've learned in this new chapter of my teaching life: Joy is not optional; it's foundational. Joyful classrooms unlock creativity, confidence, and community. And when we take risks, even small ones, we model what it means to grow and believe in possibility.

BRINGING FUN AND JOY INTO LEARNING

"Above all, have a good time." This Julia Child quote hung by my classroom door for years, bold and unshakable—quite literally, thanks to the custodian who screwed it so tightly into the wall it's still hanging there to this day. I love that it's still there, even though I've moved on to a different school across town. It's like a piece of my heart got anchored into that space, and, honestly, I wouldn't want it any other way.

That quote came to me during a pivotal time in my career, right when I was questioning whether I should stay in education. I was tired. I was overwhelmed. I was unsure if I still had "it." But this little reminder became a guiding truth for me, and, ever since, it has tethered me to my *why*: to create magical learning spaces filled with joy and passion so that classrooms are a place where . . . play is encouraged, curiosity and wonder fill the air, creativity and collaboration are abundant, enthusiasm is electric, risk-taking is not only allowed but applauded, students are not only immersed but empowered, memories are made, passions are realized, and every student experiences joy in learning and leaves school ready to chase their wildest dreams.

However, since returning to the classroom, I've learned—more deeply than ever—that while they're connected, there is a difference between joy and fun. And understanding how they work together can transform the way that we design our classrooms.

Fun is the spark. It's about energy, novelty, and playfulness. It's the game, the challenge, the moment of laughter that hooks students and ignites learning. Fun is when a student spins a wheel to see what challenge they've landed on.

Fun is when a kitchen lab turns into a competition and students start cheering each other on. Fun is when a student gets so into designing their food truck logo or TikTok recipe video that they forget that they're "doing school," because they're doing something *real*.

Fun is fuel. It lightens the heavy, strengthens the difficult, and makes the magic sustainable.

Joy is a deeper feeling rooted in meaning, purpose, and connection. It comes from watching students grow, seeing them collaborate, or having that one conversation that reminds you that your work is making a difference.

Joy is when a team that struggled to read a recipe is now creating complex dishes.

Joy is when you step back and realize that real "life learning" is happening.

Joy is when a student decides they want to pursue your content area as a future career.

For students in my culinary arts classroom, fun might be plating a dish like they're on *Chopped*. But joy? Joy is when a neurodivergent learner who rarely speaks up proudly explains their plating choices while presenting their dish, amazing the room with their confidence.

Fun is the moment. Joy is the meaning.

Fun invites students in. Joy makes them want to stay.

Fun sparks engagement. Joy sustains it.

Fun brings the sparkle. Joy brings the substance. Together, they make learning magical.

So here's what I've come to believe more deeply than ever this year: If we want our classrooms to be places where students thrive, we have to be willing to take risks. If we want to take risks, we need to give ourselves permission to have fun. And when we do that, we rediscover the spark that made us fall in love with teaching in the first place and we welcome joy into our classrooms.

So as you read on, I invite you to take a breath, let go of perfection, and embrace the joy in the journey. Have fun. Be fearless. The magic is waiting.

WHAT THE RESEARCH SAYS ABOUT FUN AND RISK IN LEARNING

Some of you may be thinking, "I'm with you. This idea of fun and risk-taking in learning is something I can get behind, but my administration may not be as open to the idea." I get it. Pressure in education is higher than ever, and resources are tight. You have standards to meet and articulations to align with. I also get that! I am there too. However, you *can* meet the standards, align your curriculum, meet the demands, stay within budget, and still jump out of your comfort zone and bring fun into learning! If you need some data to back this up, I've got you! Studies show that joy and risk-taking are not distractions from learning; they're actually accelerators of it.

Here's what the research tells us: Positive emotion boosts retention. When students are having fun, their brains are more receptive to new information. According to neurologist Judy Willis, joyful learning "activates the brain's dopamine reward system," which improves memory, motivation, and attention.[1]

Play encourages deep thinking. Researchers at the LEGO Foundation and Harvard's Project Zero emphasize that playful learning builds agency, collaboration, and problem-solving skills—key competencies for life beyond school.[2]

---

1   Judy Willis, "The Neuroscience of Joyful Education," *Association of Supervision and Curriculum Development* 64 (June 1, 2007). https://www.ascd.org/el/articles/the-neuroscience-of-joyful-education.
2   Ben Mardell, Jen Ryan, Mara Krechevsky, et al., *A Pedagogy of Play: Supporting Playful Learning in Classrooms and Schools* (Project Zero, 2023), 19–22.

Risk-taking builds resilience. Students who are encouraged to make mistakes in a low-stakes, playful environment develop higher self-efficacy and are more likely to persist through challenges.[3]

In other words, fun and risk-taking create conditions where learning sticks, creativity blooms, and students (and teachers) thrive. So next time you are faced with skepticism when bringing up fun in learning, know that data supports it!

WHY THIS MATTERS MORE THAN EVER

If the past few years have taught us anything, it's that education needs more joy, not less. After navigating a global pandemic and the rapid emergence of artificial intelligence, students are carrying more stress, more distraction, and more disconnection than ever before.

We can't control everything. But we *can* create classrooms that feel like safe spaces to explore, play, and take meaningful risks. That's the heart of this book. It isn't just about games and cool strategies (though those are coming)! This is about reclaiming what makes teaching joyful again.

So as we begin this journey together, I'll ask you what I had to ask myself: What if you let go of perfect and leaned into play? What if you made room for fun and gave yourself permission to be fearless?

"No risk, no magic" isn't just a catchy phrase, it's a mindset. One that welcomes you back to the kind of teaching that changes lives—starting with your own.

---

3   Katriina Heljakka, "Building Playful Resilience in Higher Education: Learning by Doing and Doing by Playing," *Frontier Education, Secondary Educational Psychology* 8 (January 25, 2023). https://doi.org/10.3389/feduc.2023.1071552.

CHAPTER 2

Building the Framework for Joyful Learning

LEARNING EXPERIENCE PLANNING SYSTEM

I've said it before: Returning to the classroom felt like getting back on a bike I hadn't ridden in years—wobbly, rusty, but familiar. My reentry into high school teaching came fast and furious. I barely had time to breathe, let alone map out a solid first unit. I found myself scrambling through old lessons, recipes, and half-buried ideas trying to stitch together something cohesive while figuring out how students would move, work, and learn in a brand-new space.

Classroom systems, procedures, and workflows would take time to evolve. I had to let go of perfection, release the illusion that I had it all figured out, and relearn how to be flexible. I needed to meet students where they were, pivot on the fly, and embrace the beautiful mess of starting over. It felt like building the plane while flying it. But if there's one thing educators know how to do, it's fly through turbulence. I'd done it before. I knew I could do it again.

Those first few weeks were humbling. The layout of my new classroom was nothing like the ones I'd worked in before, and finding the right flow would take time. I was adjusting to new technology, unfamiliar school systems, and a completely different bell schedule, all while trying to learn 180 names and make up for a three-week-late start. Some days, I ditched my lesson plan by second period and revised it in real time.

And while I have a tendency to want to try *all* the things and chase every new idea that lights up my brain, I realized quickly that I needed to keep things simple. The complex gamified strategies I'd used in the past would have to wait. I needed to rebuild bit by bit. Risk doesn't always mean reinvention. Sometimes, it means restraint.

I needed a plan. I needed it to work. And, I needed it quickly.

Starting over was the best thing that could have happened to me. It gave me the chance to go back to basics and build a structure rooted in the MAGICAL keys that had once transformed my teaching and helped me create unforgettable experiences for my students. I trusted those keys. I knew their power. And I believed that even in this new setting, with all its new challenges, they would guide me back to joy once again. It turns out, I was right.

I want to help you do the same thing: build a foundation for joy. That doesn't mean scrapping everything and starting from scratch. It means reconnecting with your unique teaching style and making intentional, incremental shifts that invite more creativity, meaning, and joy into your learning adventures.

WHAT MAKES CTE MAGICAL?

Step into a CTE classroom and the energy feels different.

You might hear the sizzle of sauté pans, the buzz of power tools, or the hum of a sewing machine. This isn't learning confined to paper. It's learning that *lives.*

In CTE, students don't just study content; they become creators, makers, problem-solvers, and professionals in training. They build with their hands, think on their feet, and make decisions that mirror the real world. It's in these vibrant, messy, exhilarating spaces that curiosity meets purpose and skills meet opportunity. What makes

CTE magical isn't just what we teach, it's *how* we teach it. We invite students to step into roles, solve real problems, and build something that didn't exist before. Whether they're baking bread, wiring a circuit, styling hair, or pitching a business plan, students live their learning through experience.

And I've seen it firsthand: A quiet student finds their confidence when presenting their finished dish. A neurodivergent learner takes the lead in the lab setting. A disengaged teen lights up when describing their food truck concept to an audience of staff and community members

These moments don't happen by chance. They happen when we design for them. I once had a conversation with an educator who asked how I was able to create such a focused, organized, and empowering learning environment with so many moving parts and pieces—for so many students. She further explained that many teachers she had talked to recently were avoiding hands-on lab-based projects due to the potential danger, messiness, or chaos that could ensue. She was looking for the structure and strategies I had constructed that made my learning environment work.

Her question made me pause and reflect on the scene she was witnessing. As I've shared before, the beginning of my year was far from smooth. It had been messy to say the least and I was proud of how far we had come. As I looked around my classroom from a spectator's eyes, my perspective shifted. I could see that there would be potential for chaos and catastrophe—if a structure hadn't been established. But this environment had not been created by chance. It involved systems that could hold both joy and purpose while embracing the beautiful chaos of the CTE classroom. Yes, it took planning and work up front, but let me tell you from experience: A focused, organized (and joyful) lab environment is achievable. And it feels like magic when it's created!

Too often I have had conversations with teachers feeling burdened by lesson planning. They would complain that planning felt like a race to squeeze standards into a limited block of time, stripping all joy from the process. They saw planning as a way to survive, not to inspire. But what if our planning process sparked just as much joy as our teaching? What if instead of building lessons, we built experiences that were flexible, meaningful, and fun—without sacrificing complexity?

The MAGICAL acronym is more than a framework. It's a tool and a compass in one. It's a guide for designing experiences that ignite engagement, deepen learning, and bring joy back into our classrooms. Each letter reflects what CTE does best:

M   *Memorable beginnings* **that hook curiosity and spark wonder**

A   *Authenticity and agency* **that empower student voice and real-world relevance**

G   *Gamified experiences* **that turn learning into a creative adventure**

I   *Innovation* **that encourages risk-taking and future-ready thinking**

C   *Creativity, Collaboration, and Curiosity* **that bring learning to life through teamwork and exploration**

A   *Authentic audiences* **that amplify purpose through public sharing**

L   *Legacy* **that leaves a lasting impact through reflection and meaningful connection**

This model is at the heart of what we do in CTE. We design experiences where students don't just absorb information, they live it, reflect on it, learn from it, and apply it in ways that connect directly to life beyond the classroom.

Now that you know the heart behind each letter, let's talk about how to bring the MAGICAL acronym to life in your classroom to go beyond the lesson and create powerful learning experiences.

I am super excited to share with you the Make Learning MAGICAL Learning Experience Planning System! The system will help you blend content, creativity, and classroom magic in a way that's both intuitive and sustainable so that you can create learning experiences that are full of meaning and rooted in joy.

CREATING SUSTAINABLE SYSTEMS

No matter how amazing the experience you are creating for your students is, without systems in place, you are walking into chaos. In a lab environment with many moving parts and people, establishing clear procedures that students practice repeatedly is vital. Sometimes the system you create (or adopt from someone else) seems amazing on paper but doesn't work in practice the way you hoped. This is inevitable. Keep refining until you find a structure that does work and stick to it. There is no sense in sticking to a broken system. Fix it, move on, and stay the course. Students are remarkable at adapting, but at some point, you just need to own a structure and use it consistently until it becomes routine. Let's talk through some potential structures you want to establish. Your classroom layout is unique to you, so there is no one-size-fits-all approach. However, thinking through the following checklists will help you create an organizational flow and establish classroom norms.

CORE CLASSROOM SYSTEMS

- ✳ Clear entry procedure (bell work, seating, materials grab)
- ✳ Exit routine (cleanup, ticket out the door, reflection)
- ✳ Lab procedures (if applicable)
- ✳ Cleaning checklists and team roles
- ✳ Equipment safety protocols
- ✳ Supplies and storage
- ✳ Supply station setup and usage expectations

* Classroom norms
* Posted group expectations

Creating core classroom systems is a great starting point. Using the MAGICAL framework, I've also organized some other systems that you may want to implement in your classroom These are only things to consider, not "must-dos." You have your own special magic, and, again, teaching is not one-size-fits all.

Memorable Beginnings

* Daily opening routine (do now, bell ringer, hook)
* Greet students at the door
* Display daily agenda/objectives
* Launch with a question, challenge, or visual that connects to students' lives

Authenticity and Agency

* Student roles in group work (e.g., head chef, recorder, timekeeper)
* Opportunities for students to reflect and make choices in projects
* Personal goal setting or self-assessment routines
* Classroom jobs or responsibilities

Gamified Experiences

* Daily/weekly XP system or badge tracking
* Challenge rubrics
* Clear rules and game mechanics for activities
* Leaderboard, spin wheel, chance cards, or mystery badges

I Innovation

* AI prompts, tools, or clue generators
* Student tech-access systems (devices, charging, login help)
* Quick tutorial routines (e.g., how to use Canva, Padlet, or other tech tools)
* Protocols for experimentation and trying new tools

C Creativity, Collaboration, and Curiosity

* Group-rotation systems
* Collaboration expectations/norms posted and practiced
* Digital wonder wall or jar for questions
* Brainstorming/ideation tools and routines

A Authentic Audience

* Peer feedback or showcase protocols
* Social media sharing routines (if applicable)
* Guest speaker or judge visit routines
* Google Form / email templates for challenges

L Legacy

* End-of-class reflection prompts
* Journaling or sketchnote routines
* Digital portfolios or project archives
* Celebrations of growth and progress

Once you've established what systems you'd like to implement, you can move on to planning for your content. Remember, you have permission to refine and adjust. There has never been a system that

I've created that worked beautifully without refinement. It's perfectly normal and part of the process.

MAKE LEARNING MAGICAL UNIT PLANNER

In the kitchen, a great dish starts with a plan. You don't just throw ingredients into a pot and hope for the best. You gather your tools, prep your ingredients, and think through the process before the heat gets turned up.

The same is true for teaching.

I like to think of unit planning as a kind of mise en place: everything in its place, ready for the magic to happen. But instead of flour, whisks, and herbs, we're working with standards, creativity, and collaboration.

The Make Learning MAGICAL Learning Experience Planning System is a flexible, joy-infused system designed to help educators create learning experiences that are purposeful, inclusive, and unforgettable.

And because my heart lives in both the classroom *and* the kitchen, I couldn't resist turning this into a unit planner, a tool that's equal parts practical and playful. Below, you'll find a template that lays out each section of the Make Learning MAGICAL Recipe for a Unit framework. To help you think through this structure within the context of your content area, I will explain each section.

Ingredients (Content and Skills)

Whether you are teaching culinary arts or manufacturing, there are core content and skills that you are working with. You have standards, competencies, and objectives you are teaching. If you are teaching an intermediate or advanced level course, students may be coming in with prior knowledge. And your course will have key vocabulary, tools/equipment, techniques, and employability skills that students will learn.

So, in this section you will list all that you expect students to learn by the end of the unit. Creating this list will provide you with a checklist of content and skills to include in your road map as you plan and design your learning experiences.

The Recipe (Sequence of Learning)

Once you've created your list of content and skills, it's time to place them in order. When you read a recipe, there is a reason the steps are sequential. It's the same for unit design. What foundational skills must be revisited or taught first? Where will you provide an opportunity for students to explore, practice, and reflect? When you plan a road trip, sometimes your route changes. It's the same for the unit plan. Plan with intention, but expect detours.

Tools for all Learners (Differentiation and Scaffolds)

The CTE classroom is rich in diversity. Students come in with a variety of needs and abilities. It is imperative that we create an environment that is inclusive of all who enter.

In this section you will spend time considering the needs of the students who are in your class. How will you differentiate instruction for your students? What tools or strategies will you use to support your neurodivergent learners? What classroom routines, expectations, or safety procedures will you need to teach and how will you reinforce them? What visual or audio supports will be helpful for your learners?

Creative Twist (Innovation and Play)

This section is all about infusing a little magic, gamification, or choice into the unit. This will look different for everyone, because, well, you have a magic all your own! Are you hoping to include a challenge or competition? Would you like to create a badging system, leaderboard, or a new creative project? This is where those ideas are born!

Taste Test (Assessment)

In this section you will plan your formative and summative checkpoints.

I heard a great metaphor for formative and summative assessment once and it has always stuck. Formative is when the chef tastes the soup, and summative is when the guest tastes the soup. How do you know students are learning the core essentials? Are you giving students multiple opportunities to "taste the soup"? When will you be providing an opportunity for you, the teacher, to taste the soup? Or maybe you will create an opportunity for a guest to do the tasting! What makes the most sense based on the learning? Will you include lab rubrics or performance tasks? Will you have students self-assess or peer asses? Will you include exit tickets or lab reflections? Or maybe they will keep a digital portfolio that will build throughout the semester. Assessments can be fun. I encourage you to think about how students can demonstrate their learning in innovative, creative ways!

Serving Suggestion (Final Product and Legacy)

This is the moment when students can showcase their learning. In this section you will think through what the final unit experience will look like. Will you bring in an authentic audience for students to present to? Will you have a gallery walk? What do you want this unit experience to look, sound, and feel like? How will you give students an opportunity to shine?

THE MAGICAL CTE CLASSROOM

Unit:

Ingredients:
(Content & Skills)

What are the essentials you're working with?

This is where we gather the raw materials:
- Standards, competencies, and objectives
- Prior knowledge students bring to the table
- Key vocabulary, tools, techniques, and soft skills

Think of this as your pantry: what's available, what's required, and what flavors (content areas) you're blending.

Example: In a culinary lab, this might include nutrition standards, knife skills, and food safety. In child development, it could be developmental stages and communication strategies.

The Recipe:
(Sequence)

What order does learning need to happen in?

Just like a recipe has steps that build on each other, so does a unit. Lay out the progression of learning:
- What foundational knowledge or skills must come first?
- Where will students explore, practice, and reflect?
- When will you introduce a mystery box or challenge?

This is your roadmap. it doesn't have to be rigid, but it should be intentional.

Tools for all Learners:
(Differentiation & Supports)

What scaffolds, demos, or safety measures are needed?

Here's where you personalize the learning experience for all students:

- How will you differentiate for diverse needs and abilities?
- What tools or strategies will support neurodivergent learners?
- What classroom routines, expectations, or safety procedures need to be taught?

Every great chef adjusts for the kitchen and every great teacher adjusts for the learners. Example: Offer a visual task card, provide voice-recorded instructions, or use AI-generated examples to support student brainstorming.

Creative Twist:
(Innovation & Play)

Where can you infuse magic, gamification, or choice?

This is your signature sauce. Ask:
- Can this be a challenge or competition?
- Is there a way to give students choice on how they demonstrate learning creatively by creating a video, infographic or game?
- Could students learn this through a story, scenario, or game?

This is where learning becomes an experience students talk about long after the unit ends.
Turn a budgeting unit into a challenge or a restaurant concept into a Shark Tank pitch.

Taste Test:
(Assessment)

How will you know if the learning is landing?

Here's where we taste as we go. Formative and summative checkpoints could include:
- Peer or self-assessments
- Exit tickets or reflections
- Lab rubrics or performance tasks
- Digital portfolio pieces

Assessments can be creative, too...think Instagram-style reflections, taste tests with justification, or short video pitches.

Serving Suggestion:
(Final Product & Legacy)

What does the final learning experience look, sound, or feel like?

This is the "plating" moment. How will students share, showcase, or apply what they've learned?
- A presentation? A gallery walk? A community showcase?
- A published digital product? A client pitch? A guest-judged event?
- Something that allows them to shine?

Give students an audience, a platform, or a purpose and they'll rise to the occasion!

As you explore this planning framework, you'll notice how seamlessly it supports the MAGICAL philosophy.

The Make Learning MAGICAL Planning System doesn't add more to your plate, it helps you transform what's already on it. It gives you space to infuse joy, voice, choice, and creativity into your content while staying grounded in outcomes and structure.

Whether you're planning for culinary arts, child development, business, digital media, automotives, manufacturing, or another CTE pathway, this framework brings intention to your ideas and joy to your teaching.

It's not about doing it all perfectly. It's about designing with heart, leading with joy, and planning for magic.

FROM BIG PICTURE TO DAILY MAGIC

Planning a unit gives us the big picture: the arc of the experience, the learning goals, and the structure. But it's in the day-to-day lessons where the real magic happens. Those moments of curiosity, connection, and creativity fuel lasting learning.

That's why I created the MAGICAL Learning Experience Recipe Card: a playful, purpose-driven template that helps bring your daily lessons to life. Just like a chef prepares mise en place before creating a dish, this template helps you prep your thinking, guide your flow, and serve up a learning experience that's engaging and intentional.

And just like a great recipe, you don't have to follow it perfectly. It's here to support your creativity, not stifle it. Use what works. Mix in your flavor. Leave space for the unexpected.

This template describes each section of the recipe card.

Experience: What's the focus or hook of this lesson? Give it a name that excites or intrigues.

Core Ingredients
(Skills & Concepts)

What will students learn or practice today?

- Key standards or objectives
- Vocabulary or tools
- Real-world relevance

Hook
(Pique Curiosity)

How will you launch the lesson with energy and clarity?

- A quick challenge, story, image, or video
- A question or curiosity-spark
- Industry-related story

Taste Test
(Assessment & Feedback)

How will you check for understanding or reflection?

- Exit ticket
- Peer or self-assessment
- Creative product or verbal share
- Quick quiz, rubric, or journal

Groupings
(Collaboration opportunities)

What opportunities do students have to work together?

- review or game
- lab
- reflection activity

Instructions:
(introduction/how-to)

How will you provide clear explanation and modeling?

- Demonstration/notes
- Step-by-step (I I do, you do)
- Structured talk

Creative Twists
(Gamified Elements)

Optional choice, surprise, or gamified element:

- A time challenge
- mystery badges
- Plinko board
- Dice
- digital or analog game

The Main Activity
(Method & Flow)

This is the hands-on, experiential part of your lesson.

- Practice, explore, apply.
- What is the flow of this activity?

Serving Suggestion
(Closure & Legacy)

What's the lasting takeaway?

- How do students reflect or connect this learning to future lessons, life, or legacy?

Core Ingredients (Skills and Concepts)

In this section, we are looking at our unit plan and determining what ingredients are core to this lesson. What are the key standards and objectives? What vocabulary and tools are you introducing or reinforcing? How will we connect to the workplace to create real-world relevance?

Groupings (Collaboration Opportunities)

Where will you provide an opportunity for students to collaborate? Will students be participating in a lab activity? Will there be an opportunity to reflect as a group? Will students be playing a review or vocabulary game? This can look different based on the type of CTE class you teach. Some classes lend themselves to more collaboration than others. Think through what makes sense for your content area and the skills you are teaching.

Creative Twists (Gamified Elements)

Where can you add choice, creativity, mystery, and fun? Could you create a timed challenge? Could you provide an opportunity for students to demonstrate their learning in a creative way? Could you hide an easter egg or clue? Is there an opportunity to earn a chance card or mystery badge? Do you have a spinning wheel that could provide choice of materials or ingredients? Could you incorporate dice to bring in an element of chance? Or maybe play a digital or analog game? Are you drawing a blank? Don't you worry! I will be providing lots of ideas in future chapters!

Hook (Pique Curiosity)

How will you draw students into your lesson? What will they do when they enter your class to pique curiosity or interest in the topic? Could you provide a question to ponder or spark excitement? Could they engage in a quick challenge? Do you have an industry-related story to share that could spark discussion or interest?

Instructions (Introduction and How-To)

Many CTE classes are hands-on and require clear explanations and modeling so students can practice and create. How will you provide this information in a way that is going to reach all learners? What visuals will you use? Does it require a demonstration? Will you break it down step-by-step in a "I do, you do" format?

I have found that this is often the point to which I can trace the success or failure of a lesson. If I don't make the instructions clear for every student, I am setting up my students for failure and frustration. We won't get it right every time. I am often refining each period until I finally get it right in the final hour or block of the day!

The Main Activity (Method and Flow)

The is the hands-on, experiential part of your lesson. Where are you giving students an opportunity to practice, explore, and apply. What is the flow of this activity? Will students be working in groups, independently, or in rotations? Again, this will look different in various CTE classes and there is no right or wrong way. What makes the most sense to the topic or skill you are teaching and your learning environment?

Taste Test (Assessment and Feedback)

In the unit-planning section, you planned formative and summative opportunities for students to show and share what they know. How will you check for understanding in this lesson? Will you check in with teams during a lab experience? Will you check in one to one with students? Will you provide an exit ticket or peer assessment? Will students give a verbal or digital share? Will you provide feedback on a rubric? Will students play a digital review game like Wayground or Kahoot? What makes the most sense for the skills you are teaching and the objective of the lesson?

Serving Suggestion (Closure and Legacy)

What is the lasting takeaway for this lesson? How can you connect this lesson to the workplace and to life? How will this learning connect to the next concept or skill being taught? Also, what did you, the teacher, learn from this lesson? What would you revise or change for next time?

THE MYSTERY BOX CHALLENGE

Now that you can see the components of the Learning Experience Recipe Card, let's take a look at it in action with the Mystery Box

Challenge—a tried and true lesson I've implemented in my culinary arts classroom.

Experience: Mystery Box Challenge | Scones

Core Ingredients
Students will use the biscuit method to create original scone recipes from a "mystery ingredient box" and compete in a bake-off judged by guest tasters.

- Apply the biscuit method to create a quick bread (scones)
- Practice mise en place and collaborative kitchen roles
- Explore flavor pairing, recipe writing, and food presentation
- Vocabulary: biscuit method, leavening, sensory evaluation, plating

Groupings
- Groups of 3-4 (kitchen teams)
- Assigned roles: Head Chef, Sous Chef, Ingredient Manager, and Plating Artist

Creative Twists
- "Pantry Grab": Each team gets to choose 1 surprise bonus ingredient halfway through
- "Secret Technique" card: draw one optional culinary skill they must demonstrate (ie. zesting, egg wash, garnishing)
- Guest judges: staff members or upper-level culinary students rate on taste, texture, creativity, and teamwork

Hook
(Pique Curiosity)

5 minutes:
Begin with a dramatic intro:
- "Today, you're competing in the Great Culinary Bake-Off. You'll each get a base recipe... but no full instructions. And your secret twist? A mystery box of ingredients. You'll have 45 minutes to make it delicious. And yes...there will be judges."

Instructions
(Introduction or How-to)

10 minutes
- Distribute the mystery boxes to each team. Include ingredients such as blueberries, lemon zest, white chocolate, or dried herbs.
- Students assign kitchen roles.
- Teams open their mystery box and brainstorm scone flavor combinations and plating ideas.

The Main Activity
(Method & Flow)

40 minutes: Prepare and bake scones using the biscuit method

10 minutes: Plate and present to the guest judging panel

Taste Test

(Assessment & Feedback)

5 minutes:
- Peer & guest feedback forms using a quick scoring rubric (1-5 scale)
- Team reflection prompt: "What did you learn about working under pressure? What would you change if you did this again?"
- Teacher observation notes on kitchen safety, application of biscuit method, and team communication

Serving Suggestion
(Closure & Legacy)

- Photos of the final plated scones go on a class board or slideshow
- Option to turn the best recipes into a mini class cookbook or post on a class blog
- Students nominate a team MVP and reflect on what skill they personally grew in during the challenge

Why This Learning Experience Works

The Mystery Box Challenge reinforces technique, builds confidence, and creates joy in the kitchen. It hits all the MAGICAL notes:

- ✴ Memorable beginning (hook and mystery box)
- ✴ Authenticity and agency (student-created recipes)
- ✴ Gamified experience (secret-technique card and pantry grab)
- ✴ Innovation and creativity (flavor and presentation)
- ✴ Collaboration and curiosity (kitchen-team roles)
- ✴ Authentic audience (guest judges)
- ✴ Legacy (sharing recipes and reflections)

This learning experience shows how daily planning can feel fresh, purposeful, and joyful, all without sacrificing structure. It blends the best of what the MAGICAL framework offers: authentic problem-solving, playful engagement, collaboration, and real-world connection.

And here's the best part: You don't have to reinvent every learning experience to make it magical. Sometimes, all it takes is a twist on a worksheet, a little choice, or a bit of friendly competition. When we design learning as an experience, not just a task, students don't just show up. They light up.

Use the MAGICAL Learning Experience Recipe Card to guide your planning, but don't feel boxed in by it. Like any great recipe, it's made to be adapted, personalized, and seasoned with your unique teaching style. As you keep exploring, let joy lead the way, and trust that every lesson has the potential to become a memory in the making.

Hopefully, visualizing the layout with an actual lesson has helped you think of how to use this template for your own content. This template is yours to use and revise. If you'd like to have a tangible planner, you can download and print it. If you'd rather keep it digitally, you can do that too! Whatever works best for you!

bit.ly/mlmagicalplanning

CHAPTER 3

Where the Magic Begins

Building Trust and Connection

CONSISTENCY IS THE CLASSROOM CATALYST

Two years ago, my CrossFit gym launched a 5:00 a.m. class called Sweat: a HYROX-inspired blend of strength and cardio. Up until then, I had been hitting the 4:30 p.m. class pretty inconsistently. Life always seemed to get in the way. Whether it was a last-minute meeting, a presentation, or just plain exhaustion, there was always something competing for that time slot. But 5:00 a.m.? That was untouched. Quiet. Mine.

I knew it would be tough to get out of bed that early. But I also knew that nothing—except my own willpower—could stand in my way. So I committed. And more importantly, I stayed consistent.

When I returned to the classroom this past year, I knew if I wanted to maintain this powerful rhythm, I had to protect it from day one. So I did. I crushed day one. Then week one. Then month one. And I haven't stopped since.

That early morning ritual has changed everything. I'm stronger, healthier, and more energized than I've been in years. My mood is brighter, my mind is sharper, and I start every day having already done something incredibly hard. My mornings are locked in. I'm out of bed at 4:30 a.m., in the gym by 5:00 a.m., home by 6:15 a.m. And it's not negotiable.

I've realized that the same structure and consistency that powers my mornings is exactly what fuels my classroom. So much felt overwhelming as I started my new teaching adventure. However, I made the decision from the start to focus on building a strong classroom structure rooted in routines, relationships, and rhythms. Because I knew that when the foundation is strong, there's more space for spontaneity, joy, and yes . . . magic.

Just like my workouts, the classroom thrives on rhythm. Students don't need perfection, they need predictability. They need to know what to expect when they walk through the door. Whether it's a warm welcome, a collaborative routine, or a gamified challenge waiting on the board, that dependable structure helps them feel safe, seen, and ready to learn.

Routine doesn't mean boring, it means reliable. Routine creates a space where students can take risks, push themselves, and grow, because they know the foundation won't crumble beneath them. As my students head toward the classroom each day, they can count on finding me at the door to greet them. When they step inside and glance at the screen, a slide is waiting to show them what we're doing, why it matters, and a table-talk question or quick task to get them thinking.

While I take attendance, students automatically dive into the table-talk question. They know exactly what's expected during a demo or when I'm giving instructions. They follow the routine for getting ready for the lab—hair tied back, apron on, lab job card filled out. They prep their stations, follow their lab procedures, and understand what a thorough cleanup and reflection look like before heading out.

These routines are reinforced every day. We practice them again and again, and it takes time. But eventually, I don't have to remind them. They simply know what to do, and they do it.

Just like I show up for my 5:00 a.m. self, I show up for my students. Every day. And when we create routines in our classrooms that hold space for consistency, joy, and growth, we're not just building better learners, we're building stronger humans.

A DIFFERENT KIND OF BEGINNING

Unfortunately, this year I wasn't able to set up routines from day one. When I made the decision to return to the classroom, I had exactly one weekend to process it. Inservice week was starting on Monday, and I still had other professional commitments to honor. That meant I wouldn't be there to launch the year with my students—something that, for me, felt almost unimaginable.

The first two weeks of school came and went before I even had the keys to my classroom. Over Labor Day weekend—four weeks into the semester—while most teachers were settling into routines and building momentum, I was scrambling to set up my space, organize my kitchens, and prepare to meet my students for the very first time.

Missing the start of the school year was devastating to me. The beginning of the year isn't just about logistics or procedures. It's when the heart of the classroom is built. It's when relationships are formed, trust is established, and a sense of safety, belonging, and possibility is woven into everything that follows. I was missing the opportunity to lay the foundation for the community I so deeply believe in.

Knowing how critical these early connections were, I did everything I could to bridge the gap to give my students a glimpse of who I was and allow me to learn more about them. I created an interactive *MasterChef*-style website using Canva, where students completed culinary fundamentals challenges, get-to-know-you activities, and personal reflection missions, for which they earned experience points (XP). Each mission included a video message from me, so even though I couldn't be there physically, they could start to hear my voice, see my smile, and feel a little spark of connection. When students completed 100 XP worth of missions, they unlocked mystery badges and the next level.

It wasn't the magical beginning I would have hoped for, but it forced me to look at the start of a school year, and the work of building classroom community, through a new lens. It helped me realize that a safe, supportive, and joyful classroom culture doesn't happen by accident. It's something we intentionally create, day by day, interaction by interaction. And the way we begin shapes everything that follows.

When students feel seen, heard, and valued from the very first moments, they're more willing to take risks, to collaborate, to challenge themselves, and to trust the learning process. When the classroom becomes a place where mistakes are celebrated, ideas are welcomed, and laughter is shared, learning transforms from a requirement into an experience. It is where authenticity and agency take root.

In the next section, I'll share some of my favorite strategies and games for creating a welcoming, empowering classroom community. These helped me build connections even with a delayed start—and they helped maintain those connections throughout the year.

Community First
The Magical Mystery Relationship-Building Tour

For far too many years I started the first day of the school year reading through the dreaded syllabus and going over classroom rules and procedures. Students would sit politely, but you could almost see their eyes glaze over and all color drain from their face as they feared the worst. Were all days in Mrs. Richmond's class going to be this boring?

I finally wised up and ditched the syllabus on the first day. Instead, I became intentional about getting to know my students' names and passions the first few weeks of class. I can't emphasize enough what a difference it made on our classroom culture when I made this shift. Students began to feel psychologically safe in my classroom as they got to know me and their peers. It may seem like a big investment at first when there is so much curriculum and content to cover. However, I will tell you from my own experience that when you take the time in the first weeks to prioritize relationships, it will pay dividends for learning in the long run. When students know they are seen and heard, trust you and their peers, and feel safe in their learning environment, they thrive. Nothing is more important in the first few weeks of school than building relationships with your students.

A strategy that worked beautifully for building relationships and a positive, trusting classroom culture was developing an introduction unit that covered the important procedures and basic skills framed with team challenges and mystery badges. For those of you who have read *Make Learning MAGICAL*, you are going to recognize this as the MasterChef Bootcamp. It is similar, but I've iterated it so that it can be used in any class or grade level. Use this strategy as a launching point for creating your own rendition of the Magical Mystery Classroom Tour with your students so you can create a classroom this year that is bursting with magical learning!

Magical Mystery Classroom Tour

PRINT THE MAGICAL MYSTERY BADGES ON CARD STOCK AS FOLLOWS

* Four sheets of 25-point badges
* Three sheets of 50-point badges
* Two sheets of 100-point badges
* One sheet of 200-point badges

HOW TO PLAY

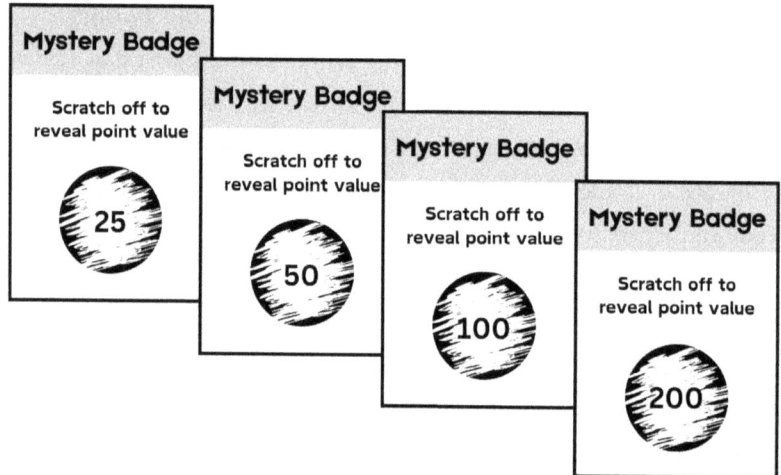

1. Laminate, if desired, and cut badges along lines.
2. Place a silver scratch-off sticker over each number. (You can purchase the stickers in sheets or rolls on Amazon.)
3. Mix the badges up and place them in a container or drawstring bag.
4. During the first two weeks of class, create an opportunity each day for a team-building challenge. This can be a challenge related to learning classroom procedures and routines, getting to know students' names and passions, or your content. Keep the challenges fun and light-hearted. Some days it can be a short activity, and other days a longer one. Mix it up! (There are lots of challenge ideas in the next section!)
5. Mixing teams each day helps build rapport and classroom culture. Find creative ways to randomly group students to add variety.

6. Each member of the winning team for each challenge gets to draw Magical Mystery Badges from the container or bag.
7. But wait! They can't scratch them off just yet! They must hold on to them until the final day of the Magical Mystery Classroom Tour!
8. On the day the two weeks are up, have "Magical Mystery Tour" by the Beatles playing as students come into class. As they enter, hand them a penny for scratching and have them scratch off all their stickers.
9. Students with the most points unlock something of your choosing! It could be a special choice for an upcoming assignment, it may be an incentive that would be desirable for your age of student and classroom, or it could be something tangible!

Some years, I created a football-style draft where the highest point holders became team leaders and they selected teams based on Google Form applications they filled out the week prior. Names are removed so students are selecting purely based on strengths indicated on the form. Each time I implemented this in my classroom, it worked remarkably well!

The Magical Mystery Classroom Tour is the perfect kickoff for multiple opportunities for students to earn badges throughout the semester. Some days I offer them to the team with the cleanest kitchen and other days I may give them to the highest scorers in a digital review game such as Gimkit, Blooket, or Wayground (formerly Quizizz). Students can then use their points to choose from a Mystery Badge menu featuring special incentives. What follows is an example of the board I have posted in my classroom. Simply adapt it to your content area. If you are a fashion design teacher, maybe they get to pick embellishments out of the "bling box" for an upcoming design project. If you teach construction, you may let them select a higher grade of wood or extra embellishments for a build. Each of us have those things in our area of study that students are always begging us for. Instead of giving in, let them earn it! The menu can change over the course of the semester too. Over time, I realized the dishwasher menu item wasn't

bit.ly/mysterybadgemagical

very popular, so I swapped it for something that students were more excited about. This is about empowering students with choice and framing it in a fun way!

Master Chef Mystery Badge Menu

MUSIC TAKEOVER — 100 XP
Takeover the music for a day during a kitchen lab. (Must be appropriate)

COFFEE BAR — 200 XP
Your choice of apple cider, hot chocolate, or Keurig coffee beverage

DISHWASHER — 200 XP
Use the dishwasher in the back of kitchen on day of choice.

MIX-IN INGREDIENT — 200 XP
Add the available mix-in option to your recipe.

DOUBLE A RECIPE ×2 — 400 XP
Double a recipe on a day of choice

The best part is that everyone wins: Students are developing relationships with others in the class, and you are getting to know them too! It's amazing how powerful a little mystery and magic in learning can be!

More Activities for Building Community, One Challenge at a Time

Creating a strong classroom community doesn't happen by chance. It happens by intentionally designing learning experiences where students can connect, not just with the content, but with each other. Games, challenges, and shared experiences aren't "extra." They are tools that open the door for deeper engagement, greater collaboration, and the kind of fearless learning that lasts far beyond the final bell.

I'm excited to share a collection of my favorite community-building challenges that have brought laughter, connection, and positive vibes into my classroom. Feel free to take them, adapt them, and make them your own, because when we create spaces where students feel safe, seen, and valued, magic happens.

Say My Name

TIME Five minutes

HOW TO PLAY
1. At any point in the first two weeks give students an opportunity to name everyone in class.
2. Line students up and have them point to each person and call them by their first name.
3. If a student is able to say everyone's name within a certain time frame, they earn a mystery badge.

VARIATIONS
* Any student who can say the first and last name of all students within the time frame earns two mystery badges.

WHY THIS WORKS FOR COMMUNITY BUILDING
* Names matter. Learning and using each other's names helps students feel seen and acknowledged—essential ingredients for belonging.
* Breaks the ice naturally. Saying names out loud lowers social barriers and builds comfort among classmates.
* Fosters inclusive awareness. Encourages students to pay attention to who is in the room, not just their friends, which strengthens whole-class connection.
* Creates a shared challenge. Working toward a group or personal goal (earning a badge) builds positive pressure and shared excitement.
* Builds confidence. Successfully recalling names gives students a quick win early in the year, boosting their confidence in themselves and the group.

Two Truths and a Fib

TIME Five to twenty minutes (adaptable)

MATERIALS
* Digital game platform (e.g., Wayground, Blooket, Gimkit)

HOW TO PLAY
1. In a digital game platform such as Blooket, Gimkit, or Wayground, have each student create a multiple choice quiz question that includes three truths and a fib using a sentence starter like "Which of the following is not true about (add first and last name)?"
2. Have the student give three correct answers and one false one.
3. Divide students into teams of three.
4. The team with the most correct wins.

WHY THIS WORKS FOR COMMUNITY BUILDING

* Invites personal storytelling. Students share fun facts about themselves in a playful, low-pressure way that encourages curiosity and connection.
* Builds classroom empathy. Learning quirky, surprising, or heartfelt things about classmates fosters appreciation for each student's individuality.
* Promotes positive peer attention. Shifts focus away from academics and toward getting to know each other as humans, something teens especially crave.
* Gamifies relationship-building. Using digital game platforms adds energy and competition while reinforcing community through play.
* Encourages collaboration. Working in teams to guess the fib builds communication and teamwork skills in a fun, low-stakes setting.

Marshmallow Challenge

TIME Eighteen minutes (plus time for intro and reflection)

MATERIALS

* Per team in lunch-size paper bags:
  - Twenty sticks of dry spaghetti
  - One yard of masking tape
  - One yard of string
  - Scissors
  - One standard marshmallow, not mini or jumbo
* Tape measure
* Timer

HOW TO PLAY

1. Teams will work together to build the highest freestanding structure from table surface to top of marshmallow. The marshmallow must be intact and on top of the tower.

2. Teams may use as much or little of the supplies in the paper bag as they want, but the paper bag may not be used as part of the structure.
3. Set the timer for eighteen minutes. When time is up, students must let go of structure and stop building or be disqualified.
4. Measure structures with tape measure. Team with the highest free-standing structure from table to marshmallow wins!
5. Ask reflection questions:
   - What assumptions did you make before you began?
   - How did you build upon each other's ideas?
   - What was the most difficult part of the challenge?
   - What are you most proud of in how your team collaborated?

WHY THIS WORKS FOR COMMUNITY BUILDING

* Promotes creative problem-solving. Teams must brainstorm, experiment, and revise together, perfect practice for real-world collaboration.
* Builds trust and communication. Success depends on listening, sharing ideas, and adjusting quickly, which strengthens interpersonal bonds.
* Levels the playing field. No prior knowledge or "right answer" means all students can contribute equally, regardless of background or ability.
* Reveals team dynamics. Gives insight into group roles, communication styles, and how students handle pressure, useful for building stronger class culture.
* Sparks meaningful reflection. The follow-up questions guide students to think about teamwork, assumptions, and growth, turning a playful activity into a powerful community-builder.

Silent LEGO Build

TIME Twenty to thirty minutes

MATERIALS
* An identical assortment of LEGOs for each team
* Timer

HOW TO PLAY
1. Place students in table groups of four to six.
2. Place LEGO assortment in paper bags for each team.
3. Display a picture of a structure made with the same LEGO bricks.
4. Instruct teams to build a structure as close to the image as possible with only nonverbal communication.
5. Set a timer for five minutes. (Time can vary by student age and structure complexity.)
6. The team that has the structure closest to the one in the picture wins!

WHY THIS WORKS FOR COMMUNITY BUILDING
* Strengthens nonverbal communication. Students learn to pay attention to body language, facial expressions, and teamwork cues.
* Fosters trust and collaboration. With no words allowed, students must rely on and respect each other's intuition and initiative.
* Breaks down barriers. Students who may be shy or quiet can shine through action and creative problem-solving.
* Levels the field. Success doesn't depend on verbal skills. Every student has a chance to lead or contribute in a new way.
* Creates collective ownership. The final structure is a shared success, reinforcing the power of working together silently but powerfully.

Back-to-Back LEGO Challenge

TIME Twenty to thirty minutes

MATERIALS
- Two LEGO bases for each team of two
- An identical assortment of LEGOs for each team (the older the kids, the larger the quantity and complexity of the pieces can be)

HOW TO PLAY
1. Divide class into teams of four and have two on a team sit back to back with the other two so they can't see each other or their LEGOs.
2. Give each pair an identical assortment of LEGO pieces and a base.
3. Instruct one of the pairs to work together silently to build a structure on the base in three minutes.
4. While the other team builds, the opposite pair looks at their LEGO pieces.
5. When three minutes are over, the team that built their structure has three minutes to instruct the other pair how to build an identical structure.
6. When the time is up, the team who has the most similar structures wins!

WHY THIS WORKS FOR COMMUNITY BUILDING
- Develops active listening skills. Students practice giving and following clear, precise directions, essential for teamwork.
- Highlights the importance of clarity. Miscommunication becomes visible (and often funny), creating teachable moments without judgment.
- Builds empathy. Students experience both the challenge of giving directions and receiving them, building appreciation for each other's perspectives.

- ✳ Reinforces patience and persistence. This challenge emphasizes process over perfection, helping students stay positive through trial and error.
- ✳ Encourages equal participation. Each team member has a defined role, helping ensure everyone is engaged and involved.

Mystery Puzzle

TIME Twenty to thirty minutes

MATERIALS

- ✳ One puzzle for each team. (The dollar store is a good source for puzzles.)
- ✳ Invisible ink marker and black light flashlight (optional, for added fun)

HOW TO PLAY

1. Write a question on the back of each completed puzzle with a Sharpie.
2. Break the puzzle apart and place pieces in paper lunch bags for each team.
3. First team to assemble the puzzle and answer the question wins!

VARIATIONS

- ✳ To add fun and intrigue, write the question in invisible ink.
- ✳ Instead of a question, you could add a bit.ly link that leads to a website or other activity to complete.
- ✳ When students give you the correct answer, give them an envelope with another question or problem to solve.
- ✳ Depending on the size of the puzzle you choose, the time can vary. For younger grades, select a smaller puzzle, and choose one that is a little more complicated for older students.

WHY THIS WORKS FOR COMMUNITY BUILDING

* Promotes shared goal-setting. Every team is working toward the same outcome: assembling the puzzle and solving the mystery.
* Celebrates diverse strengths. Students with strong spatial, logical, or attention-to-detail skills get to shine.
* Adds an element of play and surprise. The mystery question (especially with invisible ink!) adds a layer of curiosity and fun.
* Builds perseverance. Students learn to stay focused and support one another through a process that requires patience and teamwork.
* Encourages healthy competition. Racing to solve a challenge together bonds students through adrenaline and excitement.

Tumbling Towers

TIME Twenty to thirty minutes

MATERIALS

* One Jenga or Tumbling Towers game (Dollar Tree) for every two teams
* One die for every two teams

HOW TO PLAY

1. Display a set of numbered discussion prompts.
2. Have two teams of three at each table.
3. The teams will cooperatively build a tower using all blocks.
4. Once the tower is complete, each player will take turns pulling a block carefully from the tower without it tumbling over.
5. If a student is successful at pulling a block, they roll the die and answer the corresponding prompt.
6. Play continues to the right in the same fashion, with students pulling a brick from the tower, rolling the die, and answering a prompt.
7. The team that tumbles the tower first loses!

WHY THIS WORKS FOR COMMUNITY BUILDING

- Mixes strategy with spontaneity. The game invites careful thinking and quick reflexes while keeping things playful.
- Opens space for conversation. Discussion prompts create opportunities for students to share opinions, experiences, and laughs.
- Strengthens turn-taking and cooperation skills. Everyone gets a voice and a turn, reinforcing group norms and inclusion.
- Supports peer bonding. The suspense and shared challenge naturally break the ice and generate positive energy.
- Encourages risk-taking. Pulling a block becomes a metaphor for trying something new. Even if it leads to a collapse, it's still fun!

Play-Doh Magic

TIME Five to twenty minutes (adaptable)

MATERIALS
- Play-Doh
- Dice
- Timer

HOW TO PLAY
1. Display prompts for items to be sculpted.
2. Each team member rolls a die.
3. Whatever is rolled determines the prompt that each player sculpts. Six is wild and they can select any prompt!
4. Once all players have rolled, set a two-minute timer and have each player sculpt with Play-Doh.
5. Students share creations with each other explaining how it relates to the prompt.
6. To make this a challenge, everyone rolls again after two minutes. Highest roller is a judge and determines has the creation that best illustrates their prompt.

VARIATIONS: TECH REMIX
- Students take a picture or video of their creations and post on a collaborative digital platform like Padlet or Canva with a description.

WHY THIS WORKS FOR COMMUNITY BUILDING
- Invites creativity and expression. Sculpting prompts allow students to share a piece of themselves in a hands-on, joyful way.
- Breaks routine with playful fun. Engaging the senses builds dopamine and lowers stress, perfect for cultivating connection.
- Encourages storytelling. Explaining creations gives students a platform to share their thinking and get to know one another.
- Celebrates all kinds of strengths. Students who don't usually speak up can shine through imaginative, visual expression.
- Adaptable and inclusive. This activity can be easily modified for time, age, and content, making it a go-to for any group.

From Community to Curiosity
The Power of the Hook

Once a strong classroom community is established, something magical begins to happen. Students feel safe to take risks, show up as themselves, and engage more deeply in learning. But connection alone isn't enough to spark momentum each day. To truly ignite student engagement, we need to captivate their curiosity from the very first moment of a lesson. That's where the hook comes in.

When we open with an element of surprise, humor, challenge, or mystery, we don't just capture attention, we build anticipation and keep students leaning in. And when those hooks are layered into a classroom culture already rich with trust and belonging, their impact multiplies. As Dave Burgess shares in *Teach Like a PIRATE*, the right hook has the power to transform ordinary content into an unforgettable learning experience. I've discovered some fun ways to harness that power by designing magnetic openings that spark curiosity, fuel creativity, foster trust and connection, and deepen community along the way. Here are some ideas that you can take and run with in your own classroom.

"Who Knew?" Hook

Post a surprising, quirky, or bizarre fact related to your topic on the board or screen as students walk in. Ask, "Who knew?" and invite students to make wild guesses before revealing the truth.

EXAMPLES
- What common kitchen ingredient was once so valuable it was used as currency and offered as a gift to gods?
  - Answer: Salt
- Paper money in the US isn't really paper. What two materials is it made out of?
  - Answer: 75 percent cotton and 25 percent linen.

BONUS
- Let students submit their own "Who knew?" facts later in the unit!

Mystery Bag Hook

Place an unfamiliar food, tool, or object related to your content area in a brown bag. Let students take turns guessing what it is. This sets the stage for a lesson in a variety of CTE subject areas.

The Curiosity Box Hook

Set a box at the front of the room with a note: "What's inside will shape everything we do today." Let students build anticipation with guesses before opening the box to reveal a theme, mystery ingredient, project item, or even just the first clue in a game.

Flashback Hook

Show a nostalgic ad, image, or household item from the past. Ask:
- "What is this?"
- "What was it used for?"
- "Why do you think it mattered?"

This is perfect for launching discussions of interior design trends, consumerism through the decades, or cultural food history.

Pixel Reveal Hook

Show a highly pixelated image related to the lesson on the screen as students enter. You can use tools like Pixelate, Pixelify, or Pixel Art (in Canva). Every minute, reveal a clearer version of the image. Teams get one guess each time the image gets clearer, until a team gets it right, or the image is fully revealed. Follow up with a fun fact about the item and draw the connection to the content.

Debatable Hook

As students come into class, post a lighthearted "debatable" question on the screen, such as: What should pineapple on a pizza be considered? A blessing or a travesty?

At tables, students discuss their viewpoints, backing them up with reasoning. This activity provides the perfect opportunity for students to connect and collaborate with low risk and builds their confidence to debate more robust topics in the future.

CREATING CONSISTENT HOOKS

For increased impact, try choosing one of these hooks and using it consistently throughout an entire unit. Each day as students walk into class, have the hook ready by projecting it on the screen or staged in a designated spot. This builds a predictable routine students can count on, while also sparking daily curiosity. Over time, it becomes more than just a fun opener—it becomes a signal that something engaging is about to unfold. That small moment of anticipation can set the tone for the entire learning experience.

THE M AND A ARE FOUNDATIONAL

The M and A of MAGICAL are foundational to trust and connection in the classroom. Memorable beginnings set the tone and let students know that the learning is going to be worth their time. Authenticity and agency establish trust and let students know that our classroom is a place where they belong. These elements are an important part of our classroom dynamic. Together, they prepare students for all that is to follow: gamified experiences, innovation, creativity, collaboration, curiosity, authentic audience, and legacy. Without memorable beginnings and authenticity, the rest of the framework sits on a wobbly foundation. But when the footing is solid, there is no limit to the MAGICAL adventures that follow.

CHAPTER 4

Gamified Experiences

Where Learning and Joy Collide

WHAT IS IT ABOUT GAMES?

I've always been drawn to games. Maybe it's the childhood memories of sitting around my grandma's gold-streaked mirrored coffee table, laughing and plotting my next move in a board game. In those moments filled with fun and family, I first learned strategy, collaboration, and creative thinking.

Without even realizing it, I learned math concepts while playing cribbage with my dad. I can still picture the cards, the board, the rhythm of counting points . . . fifteen–two, fifteen–four, and a pair for six. Real learning happening in real time, tucked inside joyful moments.

Is it normal to feel a wave of happy nostalgia when thinking about staying home sick as a kid, curled up on the couch with a Vernors ginger ale and a sleeve of saltine crackers, watching classic TV game shows? *The Price Is Right. Press Your Luck. The $25,000 Pyramid.* The buzzers, spinning wheels, and fun-filled competition will forever be etched into my memory.

These experiences created a gravitational pull I still feel today. It's why I can't resist the game aisle every time I walk into a store. It's also why, when I began building a framework for creating magical learning experiences, I kept coming back to this truth: Games aren't just fun. They're foundational.

They teach us how to take risks, how to work together, how to think creatively and strategically. They build resilience. They spark joy. They make learning memorable.

I brought nearly my entire personal game collection to school this year and displayed it on a large shelf in the corner of my classroom. Beside it, I set up a game cart stocked with quick-play options like Uno, Connect Four, Tricky Triangle, and card decks. When students finish a lab and complete their assignments, they're welcome to grab a game and play at their table. It's been a joy to watch team dynamics evolve—students grow closer, communicate more effectively, and collaborate with greater ease. As they play, they take more risks, solve problems more creatively, and strengthen their sense of community.

In this chapter we will explore a variety of games I've created for classroom learning as well as the tools to adapt them as well as create games of your own!

Board Game Remix
Fueling Creativity, Collaboration, and Curiosity in Every Turn

I've spent more Saturday mornings than I can count digging through garage sales, thrift stores, and flea markets in search of board game treasures, sometimes finding childhood favorites, other times stumbling on games I've never seen before. Some of the best learning experiences in my classroom have started with a $2 thrift store find and a spark of inspiration.

Sometimes I tweak the rules just slightly to tie into my content; other times, the game pieces themselves inspire an entirely new classroom activity. I want to help you remix what you already have (or what you can easily find) to create engaging, joy-filled learning. To start, look for games with versatile components, like spinners, cards, dice, or timers, and imagine how you could layer in vocabulary, challenges, or content-related prompts. Sometimes, I simplify the rules or imagine what it would be like to play as a whole class. I also think about how I could involve students in creating game components as a learning activity. Below are some games that I've adapted that involve students in the creation of the game materials.

Name Five

The Rapid-Fire Thinking Game (Edu Version)

Name Five is a fast-paced game that challenges players to list five items that fit within a specific category, all under the pressure of a ticking timer. This version swaps the traditional game board for a spinner, adding an element of chance and excitement to each round. It's perfect for energizing your classroom and reinforcing subject-specific vocabulary in a fun, engaging way.

MATERIALS

* A digital spinner divided into five colored sections (each corresponding to a category and a wild). (You can create this in Canva or other platform such as wheelofnames.com.)
* A set of student-created category cards matching the spinner colors.
* Timer

bit.ly/mlmagicalnamefive

HOW TO PLAY

1. Prepare the spinner with colored sections, each representing a different category (units of study or topics related to your subject area) and a wild.
2. Split students into teams of two.

3. Using the template above, have the teams create ten category cards with terms connected to each category on the card and matching the colors on the spinner.
4. Roll to decide which team goes first.
5. A player from the active team spins the spinner to determine the category for that round. Then, they draw a category card and read the category that matches the color the spinner landed on.
6. Once the category is announced, start the timer for thirty seconds.
7. The team must name five items that fit the category before time runs out.
8. If the team successfully names five items within the time limit, they earn one point and take another turn.
9. If they fail, no points are awarded, and the next team takes a turn.
10. Teams take turns spinning the spinner and attempting to name five items in the selected category. If a team successfully completes five rounds, play automatically goes to the next team.
11. Continue playing until a team reaches a predetermined number of points or for a set amount of time. The team with the most points at the end wins.

VARIATION: QUICK PLAY

1. For a quick whole-class round, place students in teams of three or four.
2. Announce a category that corresponds to a topic of study to the class.
3. Set the timer for thirty seconds and have teams collaborate to name five items that fit the category. Teams who raise their hands indicating they are finished first win!

HOW THIS SUPPORTS JOYFUL LEARNING

* Encourages quick, collective thinking. Teams must work together under pressure, which promotes active collaboration and shared focus.

- * Promotes peer learning. As students generate lists, they hear ideas from others and expand their own understanding of the topic.
- * Invites inclusive participation. Every team member has a voice in the brainstorm, making it an ideal activity for shy or hesitant students.
- * Fuels classroom energy. The fast pace, timer, and spinner inject excitement into the room. Students bond through laughter and urgency.
- * Empowers student ownership. Involving students in creating the category cards gives them voice and investment in the game's content.

EduScattergories Remix

Rapid Recall and Creative Thinking

EduScattergories is a fast-paced word game that challenges students to think creatively and recall subject-specific vocabulary under time constraints. By customizing categories to align with your curriculum, you can make this game an engaging tool for reinforcing content knowledge and encouraging quick thinking.

TIME Adaptable

MATERIALS

- * Category lists (customizable to your subject matter). Have students work in teams of two to create a list of seven categories related to class content (e.g., famous chefs, breads, kitchen utensils) using the template link.
- * Blank paper
- * Timer
- * An alphabet die, letter spinner, or digital random letter generator

bit.ly/mlmagicalscattergories

HOW TO PLAY

1. Divide students into teams of four or five.

2. Provide each student or team with a piece of paper and a copy of the category list.
3. Roll an alphabet die, spin a letter spinner, or use a random letter generator to choose a starting letter for the round.
4. Set the timer for two or three minutes. During this time, teams must write down one word for each category that begins with the selected letter.
5. After time is up, go through each category. Players read their answers aloud. If two or more players have the same answer, they must cross it out. Unique answers score one point each.
6. After reviewing all categories, players tally their points for the round. Repeat the process for additional rounds as desired.

HOW THIS SUPPORTS JOYFUL LEARNING

* Sparks curiosity and creativity. Students must make unexpected connections between content and letters, often leading to humorous or surprising answers.
* Reinforces content through fun. By personalizing the categories, students can revisit and apply key content in a new and playful context.
* Builds camaraderie. Comparing answers fosters playful competition and connection.
* Levels the playing field. Teams with diverse strengths (spelling, recall, creativity) tend to thrive, making everyone's contribution valuable.
* Student-generated content boosts relevance. Students take pride in creating the category lists, which leads to higher engagement during gameplay.

EduScattergories Categories

A Twist on Classic Word Play

EduScattergories Categories is a dynamic variation of the classic Scattergories game that challenges students to think creatively and quickly. Instead of focusing on a single starting letter, this version uses a keyword. Students must come up with words that fit a specific category and start with each letter of the keyword. It's an excellent tool for reinforcing subject-specific vocabulary and promoting quick thinking.

TIME Adaptable

MATERIALS

* Category cards or a list of categories from the EduScattergories Remix game
* Keyword cards or a method to generate keywords
* Answer sheets or blank paper
* Timer

bit.ly/eduscattergoriesanswersheet

HOW TO PLAY

1. Divide students into teams of four or five. (Table groups work great.) One person on the team is designated as the recorder.
2. Provide each team with a piece of paper.
3. Choose a category (e.g., "Things found in a kitchen") and a keyword (e.g., "spatula"). The keyword will determine the starting letters for each answer.
4. Each team's recorder writes the keyword vertically along the side of the paper, with each letter representing a row.
5. Set the timer for two or three minutes. Teams must fill in each row with a word that fits the category and starts with the corresponding letter from the keyword.
6. After time is up, teams share their answers with the whole class, and duplicate answers from multiple teams are eliminated.
7. Unique answers score one point each.
8. Students tally their points for the round.
9. Repeat the process for additional rounds as desired.

HOW THIS SUPPORTS JOYFUL LEARNING

* Blends logic with creativity. Finding words that match both a category and a specific starting letter challenges students to think flexibly and strategically.
* Encourages meaningful content connections. The format reinforces subject-area vocabulary while requiring teams to apply it in new contexts.
* Strengthens group collaboration. With designated roles (like a recorder), each student plays a part in the team's success.
* Celebrates unique perspectives. Scoring based on originality encourages students to bring their personal knowledge and ideas to the table.
* Multiplies student voice. The volume of category cards generated by students creates a rich pool of peer-designed content, making the game feel fresh and personalized.

Words at Play
Reimagining Vocabulary Through Games

Not long ago, an English teacher asked me in passing, "Do you teach vocabulary in culinary arts?" I smiled. "I teach it every day," I said.

But I understood the question. In CTE classrooms, vocabulary might not show up in the form of traditional word walls or weekly quizzes. But that doesn't mean it isn't there. In fact, it's everywhere. It's in the moment a student calls for a *bench scraper* instead of "that metal thing." It's when they explain to a team member the difference between a batonnet and a julienne cut.

In CTE, vocabulary isn't just academic, it's applied. It's the language of industry. When a student enters a commercial kitchen, an auto shop, a design studio, or any business, their ability to communicate using the right terms can build credibility, ensure safety, and open doors. Words like *mise en place*, *torque*, *monochromatic*, and *revenue* are tools that empower students to think like chefs, educators, designers, and entrepreneurs.

But here's the problem: When vocabulary instruction is reduced to matching definitions or filling out worksheets, it loses its impact. Students memorize words for a test, but they don't *own* them. And if they can't speak the language of the field, they can't fully participate in it.

When we embed vocabulary into games, challenges, and real-world experiences, something shifts. Students stop memorizing and start internalizing. They *use* the words. They *play* with them. They *live* them.

Picture this: Instead of reviewing automotive terms on a worksheet, students are describing tools in a challenge based on the game Taboo. Instead of reciting definitions, they're sculpting wrenches or air compressors out of Play-Doh. They're acting out milestones or playing Hedbanz with parenting terms. They're sketching floor plan concepts on the fly in a Pictionary-style review. When vocabulary is active and student-driven, it sticks. It becomes a shared language in the classroom and a foundation for deeper thinking and more meaningful conversations.

And the best part? Adapting vocabulary into gameplay is often simple. Start with a stack of index cards or create something on your own in Canva. I've even used dry-erase cards so students can update and remix terms all year long. Once your vocabulary cards are ready, they can be dropped into a dozen different games with ease.

In the next section, I'll share my favorite vocabulary-infused classroom games that I've remixed from familiar favorites and tested in CTE classrooms like mine. Whether you're teaching culinary arts, personal finance, education, design, or another CTE pathway, these games will help your students build confidence and fluency and maybe even have a little fun along the way.

Time's Ticking

Inspired by Time's Up

Work as a team to guess as many vocabulary words as possible across three rounds of increasing challenge (verbal clues, one-word clues, and charades).

TIME Approximately thirty minutes. Teacher determines whether game end is based on time or points.

MATERIALS
1. Twenty to forty vocabulary cards (can be created by teacher or students)
2. Container or bag to hold cards
3. Timer

HOW TO PLAY
1. Divide students into teams (three to five players per team works best).
2. Shuffle vocabulary cards and place them in a container.
3. Review basic rules and rounds with students before starting.

Round one: Verbal clues
4. A player draws a card and describes the vocabulary word using any words except the word itself or its derivatives.
5. Teammates guess as many words as possible within sixty seconds.
6. When time is up, pass the container to the next team. Continue until all cards have been guessed.

Round two: One-word clues
7. Using the same set of cards, players can only say one word to hint at the vocabulary word. No gestures, no sounds. Just one word.
8. Teams guess as many words as they can in sixty seconds.

Round three: Charades

9. Again, using the same set of cards, players can only act out the word. No speaking or sounds allowed.
10. Teams guess as many words as they can in sixty seconds.

VARIATIONS
* Allow teams to "pass" on one word per round.
* Use pictures instead of words for emerging readers.
* Play in smaller groups for a station rotation.

WHY THIS WORKS FOR VOCABULARY ACQUISITION IN CTE
* Spaced repetition with increasing challenge. Seeing the same words across three rounds strengthens retention and understanding.
* Multimodal learning. Verbal explanation, single-word clues, and physical acting tap into multiple intelligences and learning styles.
* Contextual understanding. Students must *explain* the word in their own terms, building depth of meaning—not just memorization.
* Low-stakes recall. The fast-paced, fun format reduces anxiety and makes practicing terminology feel like play.
* Peer-driven learning. Students reinforce vocabulary collaboratively, often explaining or clarifying meanings in the moment.

Top of Mind

Inspired by Hedbanz

Ask yes/no questions to correctly guess the vocabulary word on your forehead within the time limit, earning points for your team.

TIME Ten to twenty minutes. Teacher determines whether game end is based on time or points.

MATERIALS
* Set of twenty to forty vocabulary word cards
* Timer

HOW TO PLAY

1. Each player draws a vocabulary card without looking and places it on their forehead. Everyone can see each player's card except their own.
2. In each turn, a player asks their team yes/no questions to try to figure out their vocabulary word. Example questions could include: "Am I a kitchen utensil?" "Am I something you eat?" "Would I hold it?"
3. Players have one minute to guess their word.
4. If they guess it, they score a point and draw a new card for another round.
5. Play continues until all cards have been guessed or until a time limit is reached.

VARIATIONS

* Allow teams to "pass" on one word per round.
* Use pictures instead of words for emerging readers.
* Play in smaller groups for a station rotation.
* Allow teammates to give a one-word clue after thirty seconds if the player is stuck.
* Class challenge: How many vocabulary words can the whole class guess in ten minutes?

WHY THIS WORKS FOR VOCABULARY ACQUISITION IN CTE

* Promotes deductive reasoning. Students ask strategic yes/no questions that activate critical thinking and category-based knowledge.
* Strengthens vocabulary categories. Helps students recognize relationships between terms, tools, and techniques.
* Reinforces definitions through inquiry. The questioning process naturally unpacks word meanings, uses, and context.
* Builds oral communication skills. Perfect for practicing employability skills in a content-rich environment.
* Highly adaptable. Can be played across any CTE content strand—from culinary tools to safety procedures to job titles.

Wild Unicorn

Inspired by Cranium

Teams work together to guess words correctly through sculpting, drawing, or charades. The team with the most points before time runs out wins the game.

TIME Twenty to thirty minutes. Teacher determines whether game end is based on time or points.

MATERIALS

* Set of twenty to forty vocabulary word cards
* A deck of playing cards
* Timer
* A handheld dry-erase whiteboard
* Play-Doh
* Creativity Card Key

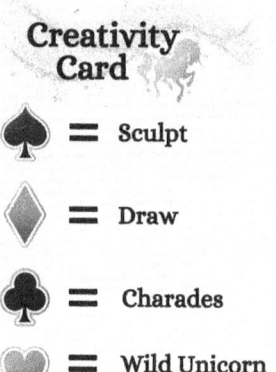

HOW TO PLAY

1. Set up a document camera that students can sculpt Play-Doh under so it will project on screen.
2. Have a cleared whiteboard ready for drawing.
3. Pass out Creativity Card Keys to tables for easy reference.
4. Divide the class into two teams.
5. Decide who goes first by rolling dice or with a quick round of rock-paper-scissors.
6. One player from the first team comes to the front and draws a playing card and a word card.

bit.ly/wildunicorncreativitycards

7. The playing card's suit determines the action (as shown below) and the number on the card determines how many points can be earned if the word is guessed correctly.
    - Cards numbered 2–10 are worth their face value.
    - Jacks, queens, and kings are worth ten.
    - Aces are worth eleven.
    - Jokers are worth twenty.
    - Diamonds: Draw the word on the whiteboard.
    - Spades: Sculpt the word with Play-Doh.
    - Clubs: Act out the word using charades.
    - Hearts: "Wild Unicorn" allows players to choose any action (draw, sculpt, or act).
8. Players have one minute to get their team to guess the word on the card drawn. If their team doesn't guess, the opposing team gets a chance to steal the points.
9. The team with the highest score wins the game.
10. You can play until a set time or until one team reaches a predetermined score.

VARIATIONS
- You can play as a whole class or in smaller groups.
- You can make challenging words worth double points to add excitement.

WHY THIS WORKS FOR VOCABULARY ACQUISITION IN CTE
- Taps into creativity and movement. Drawing, sculpting, and charades allow students to represent vocabulary concepts in dynamic ways.
- Reinforces visual and kinesthetic memory. The act of *representing* a word (visually or physically) improves long-term recall.
- Engages all learners. Neurodivergent and artistic students thrive in this playful, multimodal environment.

- ✴ Makes vocabulary joyful. Using surprise elements (like card suits and wild cards) transforms traditional vocabulary practice into game show magic.
- ✴ Student agency shines. Teams make choices, collaborate, and celebrate wins, all while internalizing course language.

EduTaboo

Get your teammate to guess the word on the top of the card.

TIME Twenty to thirty minutes. Teacher determines whether game end is based on time or points.

MATERIALS
- ✴ Twenty to forty vocabulary cards (can be created by teacher or students)
- ✴ Post-its or slips of paper
- ✴ Printed EduTaboo cards
- ✴ Buzzer

bit.ly/edutaboocards

HOW TO PLAY
1. To include students in EduTaboo card creation, give them a copy of the template and a list of words to create taboo cards for.
2. Divide the class into groups of four.
3. Two students from each group will be on team A, the other two on team B.
4. Each player from team A has an EduTaboo card. A player from team B sits next to them.
5. Without using any taboo words on the list, player A has two minutes to get their teammate to guess the word on their EduTaboo card.
6. Player B knocks on table (or uses buzzer) if player A uses any of the taboo words during turn. If the team member guesses, they go to the next card.

7. When time is up, team A gets one point per word guessed and then roles reverse and team B plays.
8. The team with the most points when the game is over wins!

VARIATIONS

* Silent taboo: Students can only act out or draw their clues—no speaking allowed!
* Reverse taboo: Students can only use a list of assigned words to describe the vocabulary term (even harder!).
* Taboo tournament: Set up a bracket where teams advance based on how many words they guess in each round.
* Wildcard challenge: Add "wild cards" where the clue-giver must describe two words at once using one explanation.

WHY THIS WORKS FOR VOCABULARY ACQUISITION IN CTE

* Deepens understanding of word relationships. Avoiding taboo words forces students to think creatively and describe terms in new ways.
* Strengthens paraphrasing skills. Essential for professional communication and demonstrating comprehension.
* Encourages precise language. Students learn to be more intentional with word choices when describing tools, techniques, or concepts.
* Builds critical thinking. Players must constantly assess: "What can I say instead?"—a skill transferable to job interviews and real-world tasks.
* Customizable and student generated. Involving students in creating EduTaboo cards gives them ownership and makes learning relevant.

Reverse Charades

In this high-energy spin on traditional charades, the roles are reversed! Instead of one person acting for the group, the entire team acts out the word together while one teammate guesses. It's fast, hilarious, and a guaranteed crowd-pleaser that promotes communication, creativity, and quick thinking.

TIME Ten to fifteen minutes

MATERIALS
- Timer
- A list of vocabulary words or themed phrases
- Dry-erase board or score tracker (optional)

HOW TO PLAY
1. Form teams of four to six players.
2. Choose one guesser per round. The rest of the team will act.
3. The team receives a word or phrase from a premade vocabulary list.
4. When the timer starts, the team begins silently acting out the word for one to two minutes without talking or pointing to objects!
5. The guesser shouts out answers until they guess correctly or the timer runs out.
6. Each correct guess equals one point.
7. Rotate the guesser each round and tally up points.
8. The team with the most points at the end wins!

WHY THIS WORKS FOR VOCABULARY ACQUISITION IN CTE
- Active, memorable engagement. Acting out vocabulary reinforces meaning through movement and muscle memory.
- Encourages team communication. Students must interpret, collaborate, and improvise, a great parallel for CTE workplace scenarios.
- Reinforces key terms in a fun format. Vocabulary becomes part of the culture and energy of the classroom.
- Boosts group dynamics and confidence. Everyone plays a role—actors and guessers alike, making it inclusive and high energy.
- Improves visual literacy. Acting out concepts often requires metaphor, gesture, and creativity, important in visual-heavy career fields like design, culinary, or healthcare.

Playing It Back
Using Games for Reflection and Growth

When we think about learning, we often focus on the time spent "doing" things like labs, projects, games, and collaboration. However, there is something powerful that happens in the moments after the doing: reflection.

I'm going to be real with you. This hasn't always been my strong suit, and I still struggle with making time for it. In a lab-based class, students don't finish at the same time. Some groups are super efficient and have lots of time to spare. Others, well, they struggle to get their cleanup done by the bell. That's just the reality of the CTE world. But I've discovered that reflection is something worth making time for. It isn't extra, it's essential.

It's a moment for students to take a step back and think critically about their experiences, connect new ideas to old ones, and prepare to try again with new knowledge, understanding, and purpose. If we don't pause to observe, process, and connect, we miss the opportunity to deepen understanding and spark growth. Reflection is the connection turning experience into knowledge.

The tricky part comes in the delivery. How can we design reflection experiences that feel meaningful, authentic, and engaging? Reflection doesn't have to feel stiff or scripted. It can be playful and active and still be powerful.

Let's explore some of my favorite ways to remix classic board games into reflection experiences that are interactive, meaningful, and fun! Because, when we turn reflection into an adventure, students not only remember what they learned, they remember why it mattered.

Operation Skill Game

Reimagined for reflection

Each "funatomy" part from the game has been transformed into a reflection card designed to help students process and debrief team activities experienced in your learning environment.

When I spotted childhood classic game Operation at a Goodwill store while on a weekend getaway, a wave of nostalgia flooded over me. Though the game was slightly anxiety producing, the memories I have are filled with joy and laughter. I didn't purchase then, but I must have subconsciously regretted it, because my mind wouldn't let it go. The next day on my afternoon run, my mind started piecing together a collection of random thoughts that had been percolating in my brain.

Operation. Team building. Reflection.

What if I could reimagine a version of this game for learning?

Let's explore how to bring the game of Operation into learning. Of course, the possibilities are endless, and I can't wait for you to dream up your own variations!

TIME Twenty to thirty minutes

MATERIALS
* Set of printed cards
* One die per each team

bit.ly/EduOperation

HOW TO PLAY
1. Download and print multiple copies of slide four and five (of the QR code) on cardstock (laminate if desired). Cut into cards and shuffle. Each team should have at least one of each card.
2. After a team activity, have students reflect on the experience by turning a stack of the cards face down on the table.

3. In turn, each player rolls the die and picks up the corresponding number of cards (e.g., roll two, pick up two).
4. From the cards selected, the student selects one reflection card to answer and puts the rest at the bottom of the pile. The student shares their answer with the team and then play goes clockwise to the next student until either all students have answered once or until time set by the teacher is up.

VARIATION: BOARD GAME TWIST

* If you have the Operation board game, you can add a twist by including it in game play. Set up Cavity Sam in front of the room. Each team's participants attempt to remove the "funatomy" part from Cavity Sam after they answer the prompt. If they are successful, that part is removed from play and they get double the points on the card. Or you can tally points earned from each team on the whiteboard when the item is removed successfully. The team with the most overall points wins.

HOW THIS SUPPORTS GROWTH AND REFLECTION IN CTE

* Promotes metacognition. Students pause to think about how they worked as a team, what strategies helped or hindered success, and how they might improve in future labs or projects.
* Encourages emotional intelligence. Reflection prompts often touch on collaboration, conflict, and communication, essential soft skills in any CTE pathway.
* Adds playful structure to debriefing. Rolling a die and selecting cards brings novelty and engagement to what might otherwise be overlooked moments of processing.
* Connects action to reflection. The added layer of removing "funatomy" pieces reinforces the idea that learning is hands-on but should always include a moment to pause and process.

* Supports SEL and UDL. Using cards and game elements gives all students a voice and encourages reflection from multiple angles, perfect for diverse learners.

Kings Corner

Inspired by Kings in the Corner

Sometimes reflection is most powerful when it's quick, collaborative, and just a little unpredictable. Kings Corner is a fast-paced, four-corners style reflection activity where students summarize their learning using creativity, collaboration, and a deck of cards.

TIME Ten to twenty minutes

MATERIALS
* Deck of cards
* Whiteboard or projector for prompts
* Small bowl of "mystery words" (optional)

HOW TO PLAY
1. Deal a card to each student.
2. The student who draws the king for each suit is the team lead for their corner.
3. Students move to the corner of the room corresponding to their King's suit (hearts, clubs, diamonds, spades).
4. Post a reflection prompt on the screen or whiteboard. (E.g., "What is one key takeaway from today's lab?")
5. Each team adds together the numbers on their cards to determine how many words their group's response must be. Face cards are worth 10. (E.g., 4 + 5 + Queen(10) = 19 words total)
6. Working together, students craft a group answer using exactly that number of words.

7. The king writes down the group's final response and prepares to share it aloud.

VARIATIONS: PLOT TWIST
* Each king draws a mystery word from a bowl. The mystery word must be incorporated seamlessly into the team's final response!

HOW THIS SUPPORTS GROWTH AND REFLECTION IN CTE
* Strengthens synthesis skills. Limiting student responses to a specific word count challenges them to distill complex ideas into concise, meaningful statements, just like they'd need to in resumes, pitches, or presentations.
* Fosters creative communication. Adding a "mystery word" pushes students' thinking and encourages flexibility, mirroring the adaptability required in real-world careers.
* Builds collaboration under pressure. Teams must work quickly to craft a group response, reinforcing teamwork and shared responsibility for learning.
* Creates playful accountability. Having one "king" represent the group adds positive pressure and peer leadership, promoting voice and responsibility.
* Makes reflection active and memorable. Movement, discussion, and unpredictability turn end-of-lesson processing into something joyful and sticky, so it doesn't feel like a checklist item.

Happy Dragon

Happy Dragon is a high-energy, movement-based reflection activity that helps students process their learning while building connections, shaking off stress, and celebrating the journey.

When I read the agenda for a meeting I once attended and saw Happy Salmon as the opening activity, I was instantly intrigued. I was almost certain I had seen a card game with this name on one of the many game store shelves I'd perused in the past and was hopeful there would be some type of correlation. Sure enough, the facilitator began handing out the Happy Salmon game cards, and I sat in anticipation and excitement as she introduced a super fun opening activity. As usual, my head started to spin as I experienced another game that could be reframed for learning not only for staff, but as a reflective activity for students as well.

In addition to my colleague's original idea (shout out to Lisa Yamashita!), I created three other variations that can be played with students or staff. I reimagined these cards with Tommy, the main character from the children's book that I created with my son, *Dragon Smart*. You can print out the Happy Dragon cards that I created or look for the original Happy Salmon game. It will work beautifully either way!

TIME Ten to twenty minutes

MATERIALS

* Happy Salmon card game deck or make your own Happy Dragon Cards using the template

bit.ly/happydragoncards

HOW TO PLAY

1. Shuffle and pass out one card to each player from the card stack. Everyone will get one of the following cards: Happy Dragon/Salmon, Switcheroo, Pound It, or High 5.
2. Once everyone has a card, project one of the Happy Salmon/Dragon slides on the screen to display prompts that correspond to each card.

3. Have each person share their response using one of the following options:
   - Whole group share-out: For smaller groups or if you have more time, have each person in the room rotate sharing out their response to the entire whole group.
   - Four Corners: Each corner of the room represents one of the cards. Have each person go to the corner of the card they were given. Everyone shares their answers in their corner of the room. Set a timer for the appropriate amount of time for sharing.
   - Sixty-second matchup: Everyone has sixty seconds to form a group by finding four people that each have different cards. Once groups are formed, they can begin sharing. This adds a little challenge and fun and eliminates the group formation from taking too long.
   - Salmon/dragon spinner: Create a spinner on wheelofnames.com or another digital spinner with every participant's name and each person the spinner lands on shares their answer.

EXAMPLE REFLECTION PROMPTS
- Happy Salmon/Dragon: Share three things that would make you feel like a happy salmon/dragon this week.
- High Five: Give a shout-out to someone who has made a difference in your week.
- Switcheroo: Who in the world would you most like to switch places with for one day and why?
- Pound it: What is something that you rock at and how will you use it to make learning magical this week?

HOW THIS SUPPORTS GROWTH AND REFLECTION IN CTE
- Blends physical movement with reflective thinking. In high-energy, skills-based environments like CTE, students benefit from active debriefing that mirrors the hands-on nature of their learning.

- ✴ Strengthens personal connection. Sharing responses related to emotions, shoutouts, and self-awareness builds relational trust, key for effective teamwork and collaboration.
- ✴ Encourages celebration of strengths. Prompts like "pound it" help students name what they're good at, boosting confidence, self-efficacy, and career identity.
- ✴ Reinforces soft skills. Activities like switching partners, giving shoutouts, and forming groups develop communication, flexibility, and social awareness, skills valued across all CTE pathways.
- ✴ Adds joyful closure to rigorous learning. Ending a lab or unit with laughter, movement, and gratitude helps students associate learning with positivity and belonging.

WHAT DO FISH AND PLAY HAVE IN COMMON?

I'll never forget visiting Pike Place Market in Seattle. I had heard about this famous fish market and their Fish! philosophy, but I couldn't wait to see it firsthand. The fish market has become world famous because of passionate employees who bring positive and electric energy to their work every day. Four simple yet powerful guiding principles are the key to their success: make their day, be present, choose your attitude, and play.[4]

Let me say that last principle again: PLAY! A thriving business that values play as a guiding principle! Amazing! My experience at Pike Place Fish Market did not disappoint. I witnessed firsthand employees who were fully present and engaged with customers, positive, enthusiastic. And they brought play into the experience. Did they just mindlessly take orders and hand fish to paying customers? No! They turned the mundane into magic by tossing fish through the air, laughing with customers, and turning every interaction into an unforgettable moment. The atmosphere was electric!

---

4   Stephen C. Lundin, Harry Paul, and John Christensen, *Fish!: A Remarkable Way to Boost Morale and Improve Results* (Hodder & Stoughton, 2011).

In *Fish! A Remarkable Way to Boost Morale and Improve Results*, Stephen C. Lundin reminds us, "This business pays a lot of salaries, and we take the business seriously, but we discovered we could be serious about business and still have fun with the way we conducted business."[5]

The same is true for the classroom. We can take learning seriously and still have fun with the way we design and deliver it. That's where games come in.

Games allow us to infuse play into serious content. Just like the Pike Place crew doesn't throw fish just for laughs (they're still running a business!), we don't bring games into the classroom just to entertain. Games help foster connection, spark curiosity, promote risk-taking, and deepen understanding of our content. Student attention is activated, our classroom community becomes more bonded, and learning becomes memorable.

When students reflect by playing the Operation Skill game or review vocabulary by playing EduTaboo, they're not just playing: they're learning through experience and feeling seen, energized, and excited to return the next day.

We can be playful *and* engage in robust, meaningful learning. I have never forgotten my experience at Pike Place Market, and I hope I have created experiences in my classroom that students also won't forget. Just like the Pike Fish Market turned a fish market into a global phenomenon through play and purpose, we can turn our classrooms into spaces of energy, engagement, and joy.

---

5   Stephen C. Lundin, Harry Paul, and John Christensen, *Fish!: A Remarkable Way to Boost Morale and Improve Results* (Hodder & Stoughton, 2011).

CHAPTER 5

When Creativity, Curiosity, and Collaboration Collide

THERE'S MAGICAL POWER IN THE LETTER C

In the MAGICAL framework, creativity, collaboration, and curiosity are intentionally sandwiched between innovation and authentic audience—and for good reason. Each is powerful on its own, but when the three c's are fused together, they create a kind of learning alchemy: a potent combination that ignites engagement, deepens understanding, and builds skills that last a lifetime.

The importance of these skills isn't just educational theory, it's backed by powerful workforce research. According to the *Future of Jobs Report 2025* by the World Economic Forum: Creative thinking ranks fourth among the most important core skills needed in the workforce. Curiosity and lifelong learning holds the eighth spot. And it doesn't stop there. When identifying skills on the rise from 2025 to 2030, the report found curiosity and lifelong learning rising to sixth, with a 61 percent net increase.[6] This is significant. It tells us that creativity and curiosity aren't "nice to have" skills. They're essential, and their importance is only growing.

---

6   World Economic Forum, *Future of Jobs Report 2025*, 2025, 35–37, https://reports.weforum.org/docs/WEF_Future_of_Jobs_Report_2025.pdf.

So where does collaboration fit into the equation? Right at the center. In the same report, the World Economic Forum categorizes working with others—collaboration—as a foundational attitude within the top reskilling and upskilling priorities for the future workforce.[7] This highlights not just the relevance of collaboration, but its critical importance to success in any career path.

Creativity sparks new ideas.

Curiosity fuels continuous learning.

Collaboration transforms individual strengths into collective brilliance.

As CTE teachers, we have a unique opportunity and responsibility to intentionally design learning experiences that nurture creativity, collaboration, and curiosity. These aren't side benefits; they are essential components of preparing students for the world they will enter. When creativity, curiosity, and collaboration collide in our classrooms, true magic happens, and the skills students gain will serve them not just now, but for a lifetime.

Over the years, I've loved creating and discovering how to fuse creativity, curiosity, and collaboration together in powerful, unforgettable ways. Some of these ideas were sparked by board games, others by pop culture icons like the incomparable Taylor Swift—proof that inspiration can come from anywhere when you're willing to think playfully.

I'm excited to share some of my favorite strategies and activities that weave these core skills into classroom experiences. As always, take what sparks your imagination, adapt what fits your style, and make these ideas your own. Because when we create learning spaces fueled by curiosity, collaboration, and creativity the possibilities are truly magical.

---

7   World Economic Forum, *Future of Jobs Report 2025*, 2025, 35–37, https://reports.weforum.org/docs/WEF_Future_of_Jobs_Report_2025.pdf.

Happy Little Accidents

Years ago, my husband and I started the tradition of gifting our kids a new game every Christmas Eve. This year, I spent hours searching websites and wandering game aisles looking for just the right one. When I glanced at a bright-pink game tucked away on the back of a shelf with Bob Ross's face staring right at me, I was intrigued.

Without hesitation I turned the box of the game, Happy Little Accidents, over to read the back, and I was instantly in love. The rules are simple.

1. Each player creates whimsical squiggles.
2. Transform other players' squiggles into mini masterpieces based on shared inspirations!
3. Vote for your favorites.
4. Earn the most votes to win!

Yep, I knew that this was a game that my family would have hours of fun playing—and they did! After opening the game, we spent the rest of the night creating, laughing, and bonding as a family. There is something magical about taking a haphazard line and turning into something unexpected. It also takes some of the pressure off. Having a starting point for creation gives us inspiration. It's much easier to create from something than from nothing.

This new family favorite gave me a whole new set of ideas that could be used in the classroom to inspire creativity, teach content, and bring a little fun, laughter, and increased engagement into learning. I have now seen the power of a squiggle in classroom learning.

This amazing Bob Ross party game can be remixed into a fun and engaging learning game for the classroom. Here's how!

Squiggle Your Learning

Inspired by Happy Little Accidents

Learn subject-related terms, vocabulary, and concepts while promoting creativity, and team building in a fun and engaging learning atmosphere.

You don't have to wait for a free class period to introduce this creative activity into your classroom. You can take this idea and use it as a playful way to review or reflect on concepts at the beginning or end of a class period too! The best part is you can play repeatedly throughout your semester swapping out prompts throughout your units of study.

TIME Twenty to thirty minutes. Time determined by teacher.

MATERIALS
- Post-it notes (or any paper square)
- Black pens
- Pens of any other color
- Voting tokens (print from template)
- Written content-related concepts, vocabulary words, or terms. These terms could be compiled by students, typed in a document and printed, or written on index cards. Including students in the word creation empowers your learners as well as frees up prep for the teacher!
- Thirty-second sand timer. (You can buy these in bulk on Amazon.)

HOW TO PLAY
1. Place students in table groups of four to six.
2. In the middle of the play area, place:
    - A stack of Post-it notes
    - A black pen for each player
    - A different colored pen for each team player
    - A stack of cards

3. Have each group pick a student to draw the first card. Game play will rotate around the table.
4. When you say go, have each player draw a squiggle using the black pen and place the drawing side down in the center of the table.
5. The player chosen to lead by drawing the first card, mixes up the squiggles and draws a word card from the stack.
6. When the lead player says "go," each player picks up a squiggle. The lead player draws the card, reads the word aloud to the table, and turns over the timer.
7. When the time runs out, all students must stop drawing and turn their squiggle drawings upside down.
8. The student to the right of the lead player goes first by revealing their drawing and explaining how it's connected to the word selected. They are basically selling their concept to the rest of the players.
9. **Scoring option one**
    - Once each player has explained their drawings, everyone votes on the drawing that is the best representation of the word by placing a turned over token in front of each team member: 3 for their favorite, 2 for their second favorite, and 1 for all others.
    - When voting is finished, each player turns over their tokens to calculate points. The lead from the group keeps tally of points.
10. **Scoring option two**
    - The person who drew the card to start the round is the judge. After all players have explained their drawing, the judge selects the drawing they feel best represents the word. The person whose drawing was selected earns a point.
11. Game play continues clockwise around the table until either all players have had a chance to draw a card, or time allotted is up.

WHY THIS SUPPORTS CREATIVITY, CURIOSITY, AND COLLABORATION IN CTE

* Taps into visual thinking. Turning abstract squiggles into meaningful illustrations helps students visualize complex concepts, a key skill across CTE pathways like culinary, design, health sciences, and more.
* Encourages divergent thinking. With one vocabulary word and many interpretations, students learn that there's often more than one right way to demonstrate understanding.
* Fosters persuasive communication. Explaining how their drawing connects to the concept builds students' ability to pitch ideas, a vital skill in presentations, client interactions, and entrepreneurship.
* Promotes collaborative critique. Peer voting and judging cultivate a supportive environment for feedback, helping students grow in confidence and self-awareness.
* Builds creative risk-taking. Drawing from a squiggle removes the pressure of perfection and invites students to create freely, a huge win for innovation and neurodivergent expression.

Squiggle Creativity Activity

A playful, low-pressure opener or closer to spark creativity, curiosity, and connection in your classroom!

TIME Ten to fifteen minutes

MATERIALS
* Projector or whiteboard
* Student digital devices (for Pear Deck or digital drawing tools) or paper and markers
* Spinner tool (e.g., wheelofnames.com)
* Timer

HOW TO PLAY
1. Fill the spinner with quotes, words, or phrases related to your topic.

2. Post a concept, topic, or open-ended question on the projector or whiteboard. (E.g., "What does mise en place look like?" or "What was your biggest takeaway today?")
3. Have students open a Pear Deck interactive drawing slide or draw a quick random squiggle on paper.
4. Share your screen and open the digital spinner. Spin the wheel to select a random inspiration prompt.
5. Set a one-minute timer. Students transform their squiggle into an illustration inspired by the prompt.
6. After time is up, call on students to share their drawing and explain it in eight to ten seconds.

VARIATIONS
* Students swap squiggles and transform a classmate's drawing.
* Use content vocabulary words instead of quotes.
* End a unit with this activity to reflect on growth and new understanding.

PRO TIP
* Celebrate all interpretations! There are no "wrong" answers when creativity, curiosity, and collaboration collide!

WHY THIS SUPPORTS CREATIVITY, CURIOSITY, AND COLLABORATION
* Injects imagination into reflection. Whether reviewing a lesson or visualizing a skill, students think symbolically and connect content to images in new ways.
* Reinforces content through art. Turning vocabulary or processes into drawings strengthens memory and helps students process material through a different lens.
* Builds community through sharing. Sharing squiggles and interpretations opens space for laughter, conversation, and connection, boosting classroom culture.
* Supports all learners. Students who struggle with verbal processing get a chance to shine through drawing and visual explanation.

✴ Celebrates individuality. Every response is valid, which creates psychological safety, encourages play, and highlights the value of diverse perspectives in CTE fields.

SWIFT-IFY LEARNING WITH EASTER EGGS

Over the past two years, I have become a Swiftie for various reasons. Not only is Taylor Swift an incredibly talented singer, songwriter, and performer, but she also pours creativity and care into engaging with her fanbase. Taylor invests an incredible amount of time and energy into finding innovative ways to connect with her fans. I am especially intrigued by the creative way she embeds Easter eggs throughout her work to pique the curiosity of her fans. In an interview with Jimmy Fallon on *The Tonight Show*, Taylor Swift shared that she began doing this when she was creating her first album as a way to incentivize fans to read her lyrics because they are what she is most proud of. Genius! As teachers, we pour our hearts into creating lessons, and don't we similarly hope that students will pay close attention to the content we create for them? Inspired by Taylor Swift's creative engagement strategies for capturing her fans' attention and connecting with them, let's explore ways to bring excitement into learning to add your own classroom magic!

Secret Codes

One day as I was scrolling through Instagram reels, I ran across an interview where Taylor was explaining the Easter eggs she hides for her fans. Something she said immediately caught my attention: "I realized it wasn't just me that was having fun with this, they were having fun with it too."[8]

---

8   Swift, Taylor. (August 12, 2025). Taylor Swift reveals insights on career, music and normal relationships with music [Reel]. Instagram. https://www.instagram.com/reel/DNQ0F6zOdls/?hl=en.

THE MAGICAL CTE CLASSROOM

Joy is contagious. It's clear she enjoys creating this immersive experience for fans, and their excitement for joining in on the hunt motivates her to continue. We can take Taylor's inspiration and generate a similar experience that's engaging for our students and brings fun into learning.

Take a look at this snickerdoodle recipe below. Can you spot the hidden message?

Snickerdoodles

SERVES: 36   MISE EN PLACE: 15 MINUTES   COOK: 11 MINUTES

Ingredients

½ cup margarine
1 cup sugar
¼ teaspoon baking soda
¼ teaspoon cream of tartar
1 egg
½ teaspoon vanilla
1 ½ cups all-purpose flour
2 tablespoons sugar
1 teaspoon ground cinnamon

Directions

1. In Kitchenaide mixer, beat butter on medium to high speed for 30 seconds.
2. Add the 1 cup sugar, baking soda, and creaM of tartAr. Beat until combined, scraping sides of bowl occasionally.
3. Beat in eGg and vanilla.
4. Beat in as much of the flour as you can with the mixer. Using a wooden spoon, stIr in any remaining flour.
5. In a small bowl Combine the 2 tablespoons sugar and the cinnamon. ShApe dough into 1 inch balls. Roll balls in the sugar-cinnamon mixture to coat. Place 2 inches apart on a parchment Lined cookie sheet.
6. Bake in a 375 degree oven for 10-11 minutes or until edges are golden brown. Transfer cookies to a wire rack; cool.

Within the recipe instructions, certain letters are capitalized that wouldn't normally be. When you piece them together, they spell out MAGICAL. This technique can be used in any subject to reveal important keywords or clues. You can create codes in directions, activities, and other written or digital documents. For example, in construction or interior design you could hide measurements on a blueprint that add up to a code. Or a paragraph in an automotive repair manual could hide bold letters that spell SPARK. In a business course, you can start with more obvious codes and then make them more cryptic as students learn to look for them.

The fun thing about this idea is you don't have to build in time for it. In fact, you don't even need to tell students there is something to look for. Let them discover it for themselves. Those who are paying closer attention will find it first. This may encourage other students to pay closer attention as well.

You can decide what happens when the secret code is discovered. In the example above, you could incentivize students by awarding them with a glass of milk to drink with the snickerdoodles when they come out of the oven. Or maybe they could earn a cup of chocolate chips to mix into the batter. Discovering the code could unlock a choice of activities or materials in a CTE course . For instance, in manufacturing, students could earn extra time with a favorite piece of equipment. In construction or fashion design, students might earn extra materials or fabric for a project. You could create chance cards that include things that students always ask for, such as sitting in the teacher's chair, leaving class a minute early, or sitting by a friend. Students who discover the secret code could select a card out of a treasure box and redeem it later. What possibilities could you come up with to bring secret codes into your classroom learning?

Scavenger Hunts

Taylor's Easter eggs don't stop with lyrics. She also loves to embed hidden messages and clues throughout her music videos, social media accounts, and concerts to create a scavenger hunt for her fans. She has so much fun creating these experiences that she also creates tiers for the types of hidden messages and clues she embeds into her content. Let's think about what this could look like in classroom learning.

Consider having a locked treasure box set up for every unit of study. I love using Breakout EDU boxes for this. Breakout EDU boxes are lockable boxes used to create immersive, puzzle-based learning experiences. Much like in an escape room, students work together to solve clues, riddles, and challenges that lead to combinations or keys to open the locks. The excitement of unlocking each step keeps students engaged while reinforcing content knowledge, critical thinking, and collaboration. Breakout EDU has an enormous library of games to choose from. However, I have used the Breakout EDU boxes to create my own games as well.

Alternatively, you could buy a toolbox and locks at your local hardware store. Lock something related to the unit's content inside with an award. Throughout the unit, hide clues and hidden messages in various physical and digital locations:

* Hide secret letter codes in digital or paper activities, worksheets, directions, recipes, etc.
* Hide secret links in graphics, photos, or words within PDFs.
* Embed visual or word clues in the slides you project.
* Hide QR codes in physical locations throughout your classroom and school.
* Wear subtle clues on your outfits. For instance, wear all one color one day and see if students notice that the color is the clue!
* Embed hidden messages in video tutorials or books within your classroom that relate to the content.

To Swift-ify this idea further, you can create tiers for your scavenger hunt:

- Tier 1: Codes hidden in recipes, directions, or activities reveal a secret word
- Tier 2: Secret links hidden in digital content lead to a photo or video clue
- Tier 3: QR codes hidden in physical locations must be scanned to retrieve the clue

Hide one or two clues from each tier per unit. Each clue is a puzzle piece that can be used for solving the code securing the treasure box. The more clues found, the better the chance of unlocking the treasure! In a recent Facebook Sunday Night Live episode where I shared this idea, Dave Burgess suggested setting up an experience where no one kid could solve the puzzle completely on their own. Students would have to rely on each other to piece the clues together, emphasizing the need for collaboration. Brilliant! If your students work in teams or groups, maybe you give different clues to different groups. They will need to combine them to solve the puzzle!

I'll never forget the first time I Swift-ified a learning experience in my classroom. My students were making scones in their culinary lab that day. I decided to create QR codes that led to secret mystery badges and hide them throughout the kitchens in various places: the back of a baking soda box, under the cooking spray, in cupboards, etc. I didn't make a big deal about anything being hidden. I just decided to watch and see what happened. I'll never forget when one of my students discovered the QR code first! She squealed running back to her team. I overheard her tell her teammate, "I love stuff like this!" I smiled big and realized the magic in creating experiences like this in learning.

Code Word

If you are intrigued by these ideas but would rather ease into embedding Easter eggs in classroom learning, think about creating a code word for each unit. Use the word creatively in written material and weave it into your demonstrations and verbal instructions. You could have a treasure box set up with the word being the code that unlocks the secret treasure. In this scenario, you wouldn't need to create multiple clues, it could all revolve around this single code word. Another possibility would be to create a Google Form with response validation, so when students figure out the code word and type it into the Google Form, it reveals a special message or link to treasure.

WHY THIS SUPPORTS CREATIVITY, CURIOSITY, AND COLLABORATION IN CTE

When students sense that there might be hidden layers waiting to be uncovered, they shift from passive participants to active explorers. Swift-ifying learning doesn't just make lessons more fun. It transforms the entire classroom into a space where wonder fuels the work, and adventure drives the achievement. Infusing creativity, collaboration, and curiosity together creates magical learning experiences for student because it:

* Sparks imagination through hidden layers. Searching for codes or clues pushes students to look beyond the obvious, encouraging inventive thinking and playful problem-solving.
* Fuels curiosity and exploration. The possibility of uncovering something unexpected motivates students to dig deeper into content and skills.
* Strengthens collaboration. Solving puzzles often requires multiple perspectives, which fosters teamwork, communication, and trust, mirroring real CTE workplace dynamics.
* Builds classroom community. The shared excitement of unlocking a mystery or cracking a code creates connection, laughter, and a sense of belonging.

- Encourages risk-taking and resilience. Students experiment with different approaches, learn from mistakes, and build confidence in their ability to persist through challenges.
- Makes learning memorable. Layering discovery with content embeds experiences more deeply, improving retention and sparking long-term connections.
- Celebrates diverse strengths. Every student contributes uniquely, whether through problem-solving, creative ideas, or leadership, highlighting the value of varied talents in CTE.

Each one of these Taylor Swift-inspired ideas have infinite possibilities for classroom learning in any grade level or subject area. By adding a sprinkle of Taylor Swift's magic into your lessons, you can ignite curiosity, connect with your students, and make learning an unforgettable experience. And I bet you will have as much fun hiding the Easter eggs as they will have finding them! So, are you ready to Swift-ify classroom learning?

Mystery Missions
Where Curiosity Leads and Creativity Grows

Mystery has a powerful way of pulling students into learning.

When curiosity is sparked and the outcome isn't immediately obvious, students naturally lean in, collaborate more deeply, and think more creatively.

The following activities are designed around playful mystery, strategic discovery, and teamwork. They will transform ordinary lessons into unforgettable learning adventures. Whether students are brainstorming unexpected uses for everyday objects, solving culinary puzzles, or connecting visual clues to academic vocabulary, these challenges invite them to engage with content in a way that's active, joyful, and lasting. My students love these activities, and I hope yours will too!

Mystery Item Challenge

Work as a team to list as many uses for an item you pull out of a mystery bag.

Creating opportunities for creativity, collaboration, and curiosity doesn't have to take a lot of time to be powerful. An activity that I have found to be effective involves an empty bag and a random item. Let me share with you how it works.

TIME Ten to fifteen minutes

MATERIALS
* Bag
* Item
* Timer
* Paper and pen for each team

HOW TO PLAY
1. Form groups of three to four students and assign one student in each group to the role of recorder.
2. Make sure every team has a piece of paper and pen.
3. Reveal an item from the mystery bag. (The first time I do this, I usually use a wooden spoon because it's something I have in the kitchen already.)
4. Set a timer for one minute and have each team try to list as many uses for the item as possible.
5. Have students select two responses that they don't think any other group has mentioned.
6. Each group gets five points for each unique answer.
7. Spin a wheel to reveal the mystery category (e.g., nonculinary use). If their use fits into the category, each team gets an additional five points.

WHY THIS SUPPORTS CREATIVITY, COLLABORATION AND CURIOSITY IN CTE

* Inspires imaginative thinking. Students brainstorm unusual uses for everyday objects, pushing them to see possibilities beyond the obvious.
* Encourages collaborative problem-solving. Teams work together to generate ideas, negotiate their top choices, and strategize for unique responses.
* Sparks joyful curiosity. The mystery reveal creates anticipation, inviting students to wonder, "What's next?"—an instant engagement hook.
* Builds confidence in idea generation. No answer is wrong, so students feel safe taking creative risks and sharing out-of-the-box thinking.

Mystery Recipe Challenge

Teams prepare a mystery recipe and work on solving what it is before it is finished being prepared.

There's something magical about a little mystery in the kitchen.

The Mystery Recipe Challenge is a favorite in my classroom because it transforms a simple lab into a lively adventure full of curiosity, teamwork, and critical thinking.

In this activity, students work in teams to prepare a recipe they don't fully know, solving clues along the way to guess what they're creating before the final dish is complete.

It's part culinary challenge, part detective story, and part collaborative puzzle, and it never fails to bring energy, laughter, and meaningful learning into the kitchen.

TIME Sixty-minute class period (depending on length of recipe used)

MATERIALS
* Two mystery recipes per team
* One envelope per team

- Recipe ingredients
- Clues
- Timer

HOW TO PLAY

1. Place two recipes in each team envelope
2. Give each team an envelope.
3. Set the timer for five minutes, having teams quietly make predictions about what the name of the recipe may be, based on the ingredients and recipe instructions.
4. Have two students prepare the recipe while the other two try to solve what it is.
5. Every ten minutes of the lab pass out one clue to each team.
6. The first team to guess the title of the recipe wins!

WHY THIS SUPPORTS CREATIVITY, COLLABORATION AND CURIOSITY IN CTE

- Fosters inquiry-driven learning. Students engage with content through clues, predictions, and hands-on experimentation, just like in industry kitchens.
- Strengthens team dynamics. With roles to play and decisions to make, collaboration becomes essential to both cooking and problem-solving.
- Promotes flexible thinking. Solving a culinary mystery pushes students to adapt, ask questions, and use prior knowledge in new ways.
- Blends logic with imagination. Students must think like chefs *and* detectives—an inspiring combo of technical skill and creative intuition.

Four Pics, One Word

Adapted from 4 Pics 1 Word

Teams work together to guess the word that the four pictures are leading to. (This is also a great hook to begin class with!)

TIME Five to ten minutes

MATERIALS
* A four-square grid with four picture clues leading to a content-specific person, place, or thing.
* Timer

HOW TO PLAY
1. Individually, or in teams, students try to guess the word before the time runs out. To make it easier, you can reveal the number of letters in the word, or even reveal one letter.
2. First team who guesses wins an incentive.

VARIATIONS
* Eliminate the time element and have everyone share the word on a slip of paper and see which teams guessed correctly.
* Set a timer for three minutes and have students work in teams to figure out the common word before time runs out. In a gamified class, you could give XP or other classroom currency to teams that solved the clues in time. Give each team a buzzer to indicate when they've solved the clues.
* Place a Breakout EDU box on each team table set with the letter combination of the common word. Inside the box is a link to a digital Breakout EDU game.
* Each unit hides clues containing four pics in various locations digitally and physically. Have a Breakout EDU box located somewhere in your room with locks set to the number or letter combinations associated with each one. The goal is for the class to collectively break into the box before the end of the unit. You could also have class teams competing to break into the box first. In secondary classrooms, you could have class periods competing against each other.
* Create a Google Form and upload an image of four related pictures for each question. Using a short answer response and response

validation, create a digital escape that leads to a bonus challenge or quest if unlocked.

WHY THIS SUPPORTS CREATIVITY, COLLABORATION AND CURIOSITY IN CTE

* Develops visual thinking skills. Students learn to decode meaning from images, connecting visuals to technical content in clever ways.
* Cultivates teamwork and discussion. Teams must communicate their thinking clearly to agree on a final answer, building collaboration and shared reasoning.
* Ignites curiosity through challenge. The puzzle format encourages problem-solving and fuels motivation to crack the code.
* Celebrates multiple pathways to learning. There's no one way to interpret the images, students are encouraged to think creatively and explain their logic.

Convince Me

Teams create a description that best fits the blot.

I love walking into Powell's bookstore in Portland. The store fills up an entire city block with different colored rooms that hold every book you could possibly think of. This particular visit, I didn't end up leaving with a book but instead a game. I knew at first glance it was one that could be brought into learning. The game came in a little tin box with a hinged lid, and on the front was a black blot and the title: Blots: Do You See What They See? Not only is the game adaptable for learning, there are multiple variations that can be played too.

In Blots, players are presented with inkblot-style images reminiscent of Rorschach tests. The challenge lies in predicting how others perceive these blots. Each round, a player selects an image and secretly chooses one of three possible interpretations. The other players then attempt to guess which interpretation was chosen. This game not only entertains but also fosters empathy, as players delve into the minds of their peers, enhancing social connection and understanding.

TIME Ten to fifteen minutes

MATERIALS
* Inkblot images (Google search or print from Canva's element library)
* Paper for writing answers
* Timer

HOW TO PLAY
1. One person from each team comes up to form a judging panel.
2. Each team comes up with one answer describing an inkblot.
3. Teams pass the answer to the teacher.
4. Judging panel selects the best description based on criteria.

Mind Match

Inspired by Blots: Do You See What They See

Teams list all that they see in the blot in an attempt to match judges.

TIME Ten to fifteen minutes

MATERIALS
* Inkblot images (Google search or print from Canva Elements library)
* Paper for writing list
* Timer

HOW TO PLAY
1. One person from each team comes up to form a judging panel.
2. Project a blot on screen.
3. Each team lists as many things that they see in the blot.
4. The judging panel also creates a list.
5. Every answer that matches the judges' list gets a point.

6. You can have teams submit in a Google Form and then project on screen to compare lists.

Connect the Blots

Inspired by Blots: Do You See What They See

Teams try to make best connection between two blots.

TIME Ten to fifteen minutes

MATERIALS
* Inkblot images (Google search or print from Canva's element library)
* Paper for answers
* Timer

HOW TO PLAY
1. Before class, choose two interesting inkblot images, and have them ready to project.
2. Divide the class into teams of 3–4 students.
3. Each team should have a whiteboard or a paper for writing their connection.
4. Display the two inkblot images side by side on the screen so everyone can see them clearly.
5. Invite one person from each team to come to the front and form the judging panel. These students will not participate in this round's brainstorming; they will judge instead.
6. Start the timer for 1–2 minutes.
7. Each team discusses and writes down how the two inkblots are connected (e.g., shape, symbolism, or creative interpretation). Encourage students to be imaginative and detailed in their explanation.
8. When time is up, teams pass their written answer to the teacher.
9. The teacher reads each team's connection aloud (without saying which team wrote it).

10. After hearing all the responses, the judging panel confers and chooses the most creative and convincing connection.
11. The teacher announces the winning team and awards points.
12. Rotate the judging panel so new students can judge the next round.
13. Continue with new sets of inkblots for additional rounds.

Content Connection

Inspired by Blots: Do You See What They See

Teams make connections between blots and class content.

TIME Ten to fifteen minutes

MATERIALS
- Inkblot images (Google search or print from Canva's element library)
- Vocabulary words or topics
- Paper for explanation
- Timer

HOW TO PLAY
1. Before class, choose an interesting inkblot image, and have it ready to project.
2. Divide the class into teams of 3–4 students.
3. Each team should have a whiteboard or a paper for writing their connection.
4. Display the inkblot image and a vocabulary word or class topic on the screen so everyone can see them clearly.
5. Invite one person from each team to come to the front and form the judging panel. These students will not participate in this round's brainstorming; they will judge instead.
6. Start the timer for 1–2 minutes.

7. Each team discusses and writes down how the inkblot connects to the vocabulary word or topic. Encourage students to be imaginative and detailed in their explanation.
8. When time is up, teams pass their written answer to the teacher.
9. The teacher reads each team's content connection aloud (without saying which team wrote it).
10. After hearing all the responses, the judging panel confers and chooses the most creative and convincing connection.
11. The teacher announces the winning team and awards points.
12. Rotate the judging panel so new students can judge the next round.
13. Continue with a new inkblot and vocabulary term or topic for additional rounds.

WHY THIS SUPPORTS CREATIVITY, COLLABORATION, AND CURIOSITY IN CTE

* Turns abstract into meaningful. Students explore how visuals can symbolize concepts, building creative confidence and metaphorical thinking.
* Encourages collaborative storytelling. Working in teams to make meaning from a shared image fosters rich discussion and idea exchange.
* Promotes curiosity about perspective. Students are invited to wonder, "What do you see?" and "Why do you see it that way?" This deepens social-emotional and content connections.
* Strengthens interpretation skills. These activities mirror real-world tasks where professionals must analyze information and justify choices creatively.

Picture This

Players draw an image of the prompt or word card drawn. The winner is based on secret criteria that is revealed after drawings are complete!

Anytime I see a game in a store, I stop. But this one is special. It came home from Europe with me! I was across the pond in London for the Bett trade show wandering through Spitalfields Market when I popped into a cute little store that had a few games sitting on a shelf with other items. The title Drawing from Memory drew me in immediately. I love any game that involves creativity. Then I opened up the lid and read the first line, "Finally a drawing game that's even better when you can't draw—Trust us." Now I was sold. I bought the game immediately and found a spot in my tightly packed suitcase.

This is another game that can be played with your vocabulary card sets too! To add an element of fun, you can mix in some words that aren't related to the content!

TIME Fifteen to forty-five minutes (adaptable to time allotted)

MATERIALS
- Drawing paper
- Pens (no editing allowed, so no pencils!)
- Secret Judge Criteria cards
- Timer

HOW TO PLAY
1. Shuffle and place Secret Judge Criteria cards face down on the table.
2. Determine who the judge will be for the first round. This role will rotate.
3. The judge shuffles the prompt or vocabulary cards.
4. The judge randomly selects a vocabulary/prompt card and without looking at it, places it faceup in the center of the table.
5. The judge picks up the top Secret Judge Criteria card and looks at it without showing the other players.
6. Each player (except the judge) draws the word shown on the vocabulary/prompt card.

bit.ly/picturethisgame

7. Set the timer. When time is up, the judge reveals the Secret Judge Criteria and each player reveals their drawings.
8. The judge selects the best drawing according to the secret criteria for that round.
9. The role of judge rotates to the left, and play continues as before with a new judge selecting a fresh prompt and secret criteria cards.
10. This process continues until a player scores ten points (by winning ten vocabulary/prompt cards, or until the time allotted for game play is over).

WHY THIS SUPPORTS CREATIVITY, COLLABORATION, AND CURIOSITY IN CTE

* Transforms vocabulary into visual metaphors. Students move beyond definition memorization by interpreting and illustrating terms.
* Celebrates playful ambiguity. The hidden judging criteria adds a layer of surprise and wonder that sparks creativity and laughter.
* Builds expressive confidence. Even students who "can't draw" feel empowered to show what they know in imaginative ways.
* Promotes meaningful dialogue. Teams talk through their drawings, justify creative choices, and connect visuals to real-world applications in CTE fields.

TIME FOR A GAME NIGHT!

Now that we've explored a variety of board games that you can remix for learning, I encourage you to play! Invite over some friends or rally your family for a night of game play around your dining room table. As you play, think about the skills that are being taught. Are you learning new content? Is strategic thinking and curiosity at play? Are you creating and collaborating as you play?

Playing the game according to the directions on the box may not be the best for your classroom, but could you alter the rules or take elements of the game and remix it? Let your creative juices flow as you think about the possibilities! Even better, invite your family and friends to join in and reimagine what the game could look like for learning in your classroom. It's contagious! Once you start playing with your classroom in mind, you won't be able to stop!

CHAPTER 6

Lights, Camera, Learn

Bringing Reality Game Show Magic to the CTE Classroom

LEARNING THAT STICKS (AND SPARKS JOY)

In a world overflowing with distractions, our challenge as educators is not just to teach content, but to make learning *stick*. Well, game show–inspired learning doesn't just stick. It sparks!

It sparks laughter. It sparks curiosity. It sparks creativity and confidence. It's the kind of learning students remember long after the bell rings.

Reality and classic game shows both remind us that with the right mix of structure and spontaneity, we can create experiences that feel both rigorous and joyful. They teach us that pressure can lead to breakthroughs, that limitations often fuel creativity, and that learning is most powerful when it's active, collaborative, and purpose-driven.

When students are solving clues in an *Amazing Race*-style challenge or presenting their food truck menu to staff and community judges, they're not just playing, they're growing. They're practicing the skills they'll need in the real world, like communication, time management, adaptability, and innovation.

More importantly, they're experiencing school as a place where their ideas matter and their voices are heard. Where learning is an adventure, not a chore.

As CTE educators, we have a unique opportunity. Our classrooms are already anchored in real-world relevance. When we layer in the structure of game show challenges, we amplify that relevance through emotion, connection, and creativity. In a world where students are inundated with distractions, we have to become producers of unforgettable learning experiences. Reality game shows remind us that with a little tension, a dash of creativity, and a lot of heart, learning can be the greatest show on earth.

So grab your stack of vocabulary cards, your mystery envelopes, your timers and buzzers. Channel your inner game show host. Your classroom is the studio, your students are the stars, and every day is a chance to create a showstopping experience they'll never forget.

EDU LESSONS FROM REALITY COMPETITION SHOWS: DESIGNING IMMERSIVE LEARNING EXPERIENCES

My husband and I have very different preferences when it comes to television. However, one genre that we agree on is reality game shows. We love winding down at night watching a show whether it's *The Voice*, *Chopped*, or the plethora of other options available. If you search "reality competition TV" on Netflix, your mind will be blown with the array of possibilities.

I find it fascinating how many of these shows speak to the skillsets that we find in career and technical education: fashion, interior design, culinary, business, and so many more. Reality competition shows captivate audiences with the same powerful elements that can transform CTE classrooms into vibrant and dynamic spaces of authentic learning. Not only do these shows combine industry skillsets, creativity, and collaboration, they also build intrigue and tell a story of contestants' growth and development throughout the season. Let's take a look at some reality television shows and the parallels to our classrooms

Restaurant Wars (culinary arts and hospitality): Chefs have twenty-four hours to create a pop-up restaurant including menu design, plating, branding, and service. To create a polished finished product, collaboration and time management is essential.

Project Runway (fashion, design, and visual arts): Given limited time and unconventional materials, designers are challenged with creating a runway-ready garment. Constraints provide conditions for inspiring innovation and creativity.

Shark Tank (business, marketing, and entrepreneurship): Entrepreneurs are prepared to defend and negotiate to secure funding for their products as they pitch an innovative concept to a panel of investors. Contestants learn how to defend their ideas, process feedback, and think like an entrepreneur.

LEGO Masters (STEM, construction, and engineering): Teams collaborate to build a ten-foot-tall tower to withstand an earthquake simulator. Collaboration, planning, and design thinking are essential elements in whether the product stands tall or crashes to the ground.

What if we approached our classrooms like producers of our favorite reality shows, designing experiences that captivate, spark joy, and empower students while helping them master the real-world skills they need for the future?

BINGE-WATCHING TURNS INTO AN EPIPHANY

Over a winter break, I found myself binge-watching the Netflix global cooking competition series *The Final Table*. What began as a cozy day in pajamas quickly turned into an epiphany that forever changed how I looked at lesson design. As the show unfolded, I realized I wasn't just watching it for fun; I was watching it through the lens of a lesson designer. The structure, drama, and emotion of the show mirrored everything I believe learning can and should be.

In the show, twelve teams of chefs from around the world competed to re-create and reimagine iconic dishes from various countries. Each episode focused on one nation, with a national dish selected by cultural ambassadors for the chefs to interpret. The lowest-scoring teams faced off in a second challenge called the final plate, where they had to center their dish around a surprise local ingredient selected by a renowned chef from that country. Everything about the show was intentional, immersive, and rich with storytelling, just like our most powerful lessons.

What if we approached our classrooms like the producers of *The Final Table*? What if we infused the same structure, intentionality, and opportunities for performance into our learning environments? Here's what this show, and so many other reality competition shows, can teach us.

Set the stage with a dramatic opening. From the moment *The Final Table* begins, viewers are pulled in through dynamic lighting, cinematic music, and emotionally compelling introductions. The stakes feel high, and the anticipation is tangible. In our classrooms, we have to compete with countless distractions. A strong "hook" is essential. Whether it's dimming the lights, playing suspenseful music, hiding a mystery box under a cloth, or launching a teaser video, setting the scene creates curiosity and primes the brain for learning. As Dave Burgess says in *Teach Like a PIRATE*, "Standing out from the crowd is the only way to guarantee your message is received in a culture that is increasingly distracted."[9]

Deliver clear, compelling expectations. Each challenge on the show begins with a crystal-clear explanation of what's expected. The judges articulate not just the *what* but the *why*, setting high standards and a clear road map for success. This is our responsibility too. Mystery and surprise are great in lesson delivery. However, standards and expectations should never be confusing. We must communicate learning

---

9 Burgess, Dave. *Teach Like a PIRATE: Increase Student Engagement, Boost Your Creativity, and Transform Your Life as an Educator* (Dave Burgess Consulting, 2012), 28.

targets and success criteria in a way students can own. In my class, students know exactly what the objective and overarching plan is when they walk into the room and glance at the screen. I am intentional about communicating why we are doing what we are doing and what they are expected to learn. High expectations don't have to be intimidating; they can be empowering when paired with clarity.

Foster meaningful collaboration. The chef duos on *The Final Table* work like well-oiled machines. They are communicating constantly, adjusting in real time, and leaning into one another's strengths. Their success depends on trust and synergy. In education, collaboration is often an afterthought. But when we intentionally build classroom cultures rooted in relationships and trust, teamwork becomes a powerful learning strategy. Assigning roles, offering feedback protocols, and celebrating collective wins helps students understand that success is rarely a solo effort.

Challenge critical thinking. The time constraints, unfamiliar ingredients, and high expectations push the contestants beyond routine execution. They have to *think*. They tap into prior knowledge, adapt techniques, and solve problems in real time. We should design learning that stretches students beyond recall. The most effective challenges are those where students are so immersed in solving the problem, they forget how hard they're thinking. That's when learning sticks.

Embrace creativity with constraints. Give a professional chef unlimited time, ingredients, and resources, and they'll probably make something great. But give them sixty minutes, a narrow list of ingredients, and a bold theme? Now *that* takes imagination. The same applies to students. When we give them just enough structure to guide their thinking and the freedom to create within boundaries, they surprise us every time. A focused objective and a ticking clock can often unlock more originality than total freedom.

Encourage calculated risks. Throughout the show, chefs had to make high-stakes decisions: Should they attempt a complex technique? Plate a dish differently than expected? Feature a less familiar ingredient?

Risk-taking is essential in both cooking and learning. As educators, we must model this by trying new approaches, embracing iteration, and inviting students to do the same. Learning flourishes when students feel safe to fail, revise, and try again, just like the chefs on that global stage.

Create an authentic audience. One of the most powerful elements of *The Final Table* is the presence of esteemed judges. The chefs aren't just cooking for a grade, they're presenting their creations to people they respect, admire, and want to impress. And their reflection, their explanation of process and technique, matters just as much as the dish itself. I have seen such power in bringing in guests, whether they are school and district office staff, local professionals, or Zoom guests, so I look for opportunities in every unit to bring in folks from outside the class. When we give students a real audience, it transforms their mindset. They care more. They try harder. They shine brighter. Because their learning matters beyond the classroom walls.

WHY REALITY AND GAME SHOWS WORK IN EDUCATION

There's a reason we find ourselves glued to the edge of our seats during reality competition shows and traditional game shows. The drama. The pressure. The creativity. The celebration when someone pulls off the impossible in the final seconds. These shows captivate us because they tap into the core of what drives human motivation: urgency, agency, and anticipation. Those same elements can make learning unforgettable in the CTE classroom.

CTE classrooms are already hands-on, skill-focused, and project-driven, which makes them the perfect environment to bring game show–style learning to life. When students are immersed in a challenge that mirrors a high-stakes competition like *Chopped* or *Shark Tank*, they're not just "doing school," they're stepping into roles that mirror real careers, real challenges, and real growth.

Game show–inspired learning works because it activates multiple regions of the brain. According to neurologist Judy Willis, joyful learning "activates the brain's dopamine reward system," which improves memory, motivation, and attention.[10] This means that when students are laughing, moving, collaborating, and competing (even in low-stakes ways), their brains are actually primed to retain what they're learning.

What these shows do brilliantly is structure unpredictability. There are rules, goals, and boundaries, but within them lies space for creativity, authenticity, and choice. Contestants make real decisions that reflect their unique strengths, perspectives, and styles. They think critically, problem-solve, and innovate while staying true to who they are. In education, this is gold! When we design learning with that same balance of structure and freedom, we create a framework where students can take risks, explore authentic challenges, and exercise agency without fear of failure, because the format itself celebrates trying, adapting, and trying again.

Reality game shows also masterfully weave in an authentic audience of judges and industry professionals to offer guidance, feedback, and encouragement. In the singing competition *The Voice*, contestants are provided a coach to mentor them and prepare them for the vocal challenges ahead. In *Next Level Chef*, contestants work alongside celebrity chefs who guide them in the midst of competition, while a panel of judges delivers thoughtful critique and feedback after each dish is presented. Throughout each leg of *The Amazing Race*, locals appear at various checkpoints to provide immersive cultural experiences and challenges. Though each reality competition engages its audience in different ways, without these experts and authentic voices, the show would lose its depth, credibility, and connection to the real world.

When we intentionally and thoughtfully layer these elements into our lesson design, something magical happens. Students don't just complete assignments, they step into roles. They collaborate, take risks,

---

10 Willis, Judy. "The Neuroscience of Joyful Education," Association of Supervision and Curriculum Development 64 (June 1, 2007). https://www.ascd.org/el/articles/the-neuroscience-of-joyful-education.

persevere, and showcase their growth. They become empowered learners. And our classrooms? They become vibrant, purpose-filled spaces where joy and passion reside.

TRANSLATING TV MAGIC INTO LEARNING MAGIC: DESIGNING YOUR OWN GAME SHOW CHALLENGE

There is a lot we can learn from televised competitions if we're willing to tune in, take notes, and translate it into classroom magic. But it can feel much more overwhelming to translate *Project Runway* for the classroom than it can, say, a board game like Scattergories. Luckily, turning a reality competition show into a classroom challenge isn't about copying the show entirely. It's about stealing the structure and then translating the pacing, energy, and collaborative pressure into a learning experience that builds both technical and transferable skills.

The key is to think in terms of show-to-skill mapping: Which show aligns with the skill or behavior I want students to develop? Which elements of that show can I bring into the classroom to make learning more memorable, meaningful, and motivating?

Let's break down a few examples:

Reality/ Game Show	What It Models	CTE Skill Tie-In
Chopped	Improvisation, time management, creativity	Culinary arts, lab skills, food truck concepts
Shark Tank	Entrepreneurial thinking, pitching, finance	Marketing, business, entrepreneurship
Project Runway	Iteration, design process, presentation	Fashion design, interior design, feedback loops
The Amazing Race	Sequencing, critical thinking, teamwork	Multistep tasks, problem-solving, labs
Jeopardy!	Quick recall, review, category thinking	Vocabulary, test prep, unit review

The Price Is Right	Estimation, budgeting, consumer knowledge	Menu planning, purchasing, interior cost outs
Nailed It!	Growth mindset, embracing imperfection	Skill-building, first drafts, creativity

Remember, the magic doesn't come from the TV show itself, it comes from how you remix it. Whether you're creating a five-minute review game or an immersive multiday competition, the process of building your own classroom challenge from a game show format can be both simple and incredibly rewarding.

Here's a step-by-step guide to bringing your own game show challenge to life:

Step One: Choose Your Show Inspiration

Ask yourself: What kind of energy or structure do I want to bring into the room today?

- A fast-paced, adrenaline-pumping task: *The Amazing Race*
- A chance to showcase presentation and persuasion: *Shark Tank*
- A surprise twist that builds problem-solving and resilience: *Chopped* or *Nailed It!*
- A reflective, slow burn with a creative end product: *Project Runway*

Once you've picked your format, it becomes your blueprint.

Step Two: Define the Skill Focus

What do you want students to learn, demonstrate, or reflect on?

Your challenge should align with your content standards and technical skills but also layer in soft skills like collaboration, creativity, critical thinking, time management, and adaptability.

For example:

* Culinary arts: knife cuts, mise en place, flavor balancing, plating
* Fashion design: sketching, construction, upcycling, client-need analysis
* Business/marketing: pitching, market research, budgeting, branding
* Construction: blueprint reading, safety procedures, tool selection

Let your desired outcome guide the challenge format.

Step Three: Add a Twist

Every great game show has a twist: a surprise ingredient, a secret task, or a rule change midway through. These unexpected elements create excitement and push students to think on their feet.

Twist ideas:

* Limited materials (only use what's in your station's basket)
* Time penalty or bonus for specific tasks
* A mystery element (ingredient, client request, design detail)
* Teams can "buy" features they like—but you lose time if you go over budget
* Teams can earn "immunity" or "bonus time" through minichallenges

These twists mimic real-world curve balls and build creative confidence.

Step Four: Build the Set

This doesn't have to be a Hollywood-level production, however some light staging and props make a big impact!

* Use music, lighting, buzzers, or timers to set the mood.

- ✳ Create cards, clue envelopes, or digital wheels (like wheelofnames.com) for random elements.
- ✳ Use whiteboards, Play-Doh, props, or Canva slides to mimic game elements.
- ✳ Give each team a role: chef, project manager, communicator, presenter.
- ✳ Create signage or visuals to brand your game ("Welcome to Culinary Feud!").

Even simple touches can transport students into the world of the challenge.

Step Five: Run It Live (or Asynchronously)

Let the challenge unfold. Observe student collaboration, thinking, and performance. Depending on the complexity, you may:

- ✳ Build in checkpoints where students reflect or self-assess.
- ✳ Use rubrics for peer, self, and teacher feedback.
- ✳ Include a debrief discussion to unpack what worked, what didn't, and what was learned.

You can even capture the experience on video or social media to showcase student creativity and celebrate learning publicly.

Tips for Game Show Challenges

Here's are some additional tips to keep in mind when bringing your challenge to life.

Plan with intention. Game shows are fun, but they're also purposeful. Design your challenge around the skills and content you want students to practice. It's a bonus if they also build in collaboration, communication, or real-world relevance.

Let go of perfection. Just like the contestants on *Nailed It!*, you don't need to get everything right the first time. Test, tweak, and reflect. Your students will love the creativity, even if the buzzers break or the timer glitches.

Build in roles. Assign team roles like captain, clue keeper, time manager, or presenter. It increases equity, distributes responsibility, and supports neurodivergent learners who thrive with structure.

Be the host. Channel your inner game show host! Add a little dramatic flair, play theme music, wear a fun hat, or use a catchphrase. Your energy sets the tone and helps build a joyful, fearless learning culture.

Keep it flexible. You don't need a full class period or all the bells and whistles. You can even turn a worksheet review into a *Pyramid*-style guessing game or a *Price Is Right* game to assess content knowledge. Start small, build momentum, and watch the magic unfold.

In the next section, I'll offer some examples of how I've remixed reality competition and game shows to meet particular needs in my classroom. What will your remix look like?

The Chopped Challenge

Inspired by the hit Food Network show *Chopped,* this challenge infuses creativity, technique, and teamwork and a mystery basket of ingredients. Teams of students are required to create a cohesive dish with the provided ingredients within the set time limit.

TIME Thirty to sixty minutes (time will vary based on challenge, and your class length)

MATERIALS

- A basket, box, or bowl of mystery ingredients
- Additional pantry items that could be used to prepare a dish
- Utensils/equipment needed to prepare mystery ingredients

HOW TO PLAY

1. Each team opens a box/basket of three or four mystery ingredients.
2. Teams have five minutes to discuss their plan and how they'll incorporate all the required ingredients into a dish.
3. Teams prepare their dishes using available pantry items, showcasing creativity and culinary technique.
4. Students plate and present their dishes to judges (staff, peers, or guest chefs), explaining their concept, techniques, and flavor choices.
5. After judging, or in a following class period, students reflect on teamwork, time management, problem-solving, and what they'd do differently next time.

VARIATIONS

- Interior Design: The mystery box contains unexpected materials, paint swatches, and a design brief. Students create a cohesive concept board or mock up using the required materials and colors.
- Fashion Design: The mystery box contains materials. Students design and construct a garment or accessory that meets a given theme.
- Construction: The mystery box contains construction materials (e.g., wood pieces, metal, screws, nails, etc.). Students create a mini piece of furniture using the materials given.

WHY THIS SUPPORTS MAGICAL LEARNING

- Working within limits inspires innovative thinking and problem-solving
- Encourages collaboration and teamwork to create cohesive dish
- Taking ownership of roles fosters confidence and authenticity
- Hands-on, authentic experiences expand students' technical and academic vocabulary

* Real-world, career-connected learning experiences promote authenticity and prepare students for success beyond the classroom

Shark Tank Challenge

Modeled after the hit show *Shark Tank*, this challenge invites students to step into the role of entrepreneurs pitching their big ideas to a panel of "investors." Whether it's a new product, service, or food concept, students must craft a compelling presentation that combines creativity, market research, and persuasive communication.

In this challenge, students develop a business concept from the ground up, naming their company, designing a logo or prototype, determining costs and pricing, and outlining a marketing strategy. Then, they pitch their ideas to a panel of "Sharks" (teachers, administrators, or community business leaders) who will ask tough questions and decide which ideas deserve an "investment."

TIME One to two weeks

MATERIALS
* Presentation platform

HOW TO PLAY
1. Brainstorm and concept development (one or two class periods): Students or teams identify a product or service that solves a real problem or meets a market need.
2. Business Plan Creation (one class period): Students outline their target audience, cost structure, pricing, brand identity, and promotional plan.
3. Pitch Prep (one class period): Teams design a visual pitch deck (slides, poster, or prototype) and rehearse their presentation.

4. Pitch Day (one class period): Teams deliver their three-to-five-minute pitch to the panel, followed by a brief Q and A. Sharks may "invest," offer feedback, or negotiate terms.
5. Reflection: Students reflect on what went well, what they'd revise, and how they'd move forward in a real business environment.

VARIATIONS
- Each team draws a challenge card that changes the market (e.g., "A new competitor enters" or "You lose your main supplier").
- A team can earn an "extra minute to pitch" by completing a business-trivia minichallenge.
- The Sharks choose one team to "revise and re-pitch" based on feedback for a bonus investment.

WHY THIS SUPPORTS MAGICAL LEARNING
- Engaging in an authentic scenario allows students to connect classroom learning to real-world business practices, strengthening their understanding of how ideas become viable business ventures.
- Collaborative challenges require students to share ideas, problem-solve strategically, and support one another, mirroring the interpersonal dynamics of successful professional teams.
- Presenting ideas in a high-energy, time-sensitive environment helps students refine their communication, think on their feet, and respond confidently to feedback.
- Through iterative idea development, students learn the importance of creativity, constructive critique, and compromise—skills essential to thriving in both industry and everyday life.

Amazing Race Challenge

The Amazing Race Challenge is a fast-paced, team-based activity modeled after *The Amazing Race*. Students rotate through a series of four skill-focused stations designed to strengthen essential CTE competencies such as organization, accuracy, teamwork, and efficiency. Each station reinforces workplace-readiness skills through hands-on, timed challenges that simulate real-world problem-solving.

TIME Sixty minutes (time can be adjusted)

MATERIALS
* Station cards (one per station)
* Station supplies (based on content area)
    * Culinary: measuring tools, ingredients, sanitizing supplies
    * Design: rulers, swatches, tools, design templates
    * Health science: lab kits, safety gear, task cards
* Team recording sheets or rubrics
* Stopwatch or timer

HOW TO PLAY
1. Divide students into teams of three or four and explain the challenge: Each team will race to complete four stations focused on essential workplace skills.
2. Distribute the first task card to each team and start the timer.
3. Teams complete the task, have it checked by the instructor or judge, and then receive the next clue or station card.
4. Continue until all teams have completed every station.
5. Teams earn points for accuracy, teamwork, efficiency, and professionalism.
6. Facilitate a reflection about which skills were used, challenges faced, and how this mirrors real-world tasks in their CTE pathway

VARIATIONS

* Content customization: Tailor each station to your pathway (e.g., measuring accuracy for culinary, blueprint reading for interior design or architecture, patient procedure setup for Health Science).
* Digital race: Use QR codes for digital tasks/clues or virtual submissions.
* Career connection: Rename stations after real industry roles or workplace departments.
* Leadership rotation: Have students rotate leadership roles at each station to emphasize communication and management skills.
* Mystery round: Add a bonus round with an unexpected challenge that tests adaptability.

WHY THIS SUPPORTS MAGICAL LEARNING

* Students make real-time choices, solve problems collaboratively, and take responsibility for how their team performs, fostering confidence and accountability.
* Timed challenges, task cards, and friendly competition simulate workplace demands while keeping the experience fun, motivating, and engaging.
* Students think on their feet, adapt strategies at each station, and discuss multiple ways to achieve success, nurturing flexibility, and innovation.
* Teams must communicate clearly, delegate tasks, and collaborate efficiently, developing essential interpersonal skills for both school and career success.

The Cutthroat Challenge

Reality game shows often captivate us with their high-stakes drama and unexpected twists. One such show, *Cutthroat Kitchen*, hosted by Alton Brown, features chefs bidding to sabotage their competitors while trying to create culinary masterpieces. Inspired by this concept, I transformed my culinary arts classroom into a battleground of strategy, creativity, and resilience. Students complete a hands-on project or lab while navigating intentional "twists," or obstacles that simulate real-world workplace challenges. Whether it's limited resources, time constraints, or unexpected curve balls, students must think critically, adapt quickly, and maintain quality under pressure, just like professionals in their CTE field.

TIME Sixty to seventy minutes

MATERIALS
- Core project or lab materials (based on content area)
    - Culinary: recipe ingredients, kitchen tools
    - Interior design: design materials, color swatches, drafting tools
    - Health science: lab equipment, patient scenarios, supply kits
    - Business/marketing: product samples, budget sheets, presentation materials
- "Sabotage" or "Twist" cards (printed or digital)
- Play money, tokens, or digital currency for bidding (optional)
- Scoring rubric or judging sheet
- Timer

HOW TO PLAY
1. Explain that students will complete a hands-on project or lab while navigating real-world constraints and challenges.
2. Provide all teams the same base materials or supplies.
3. Give each team a set amount of "money" or points.

4. Present a few "twists" (e.g., swap tools, work with your nondominant hand, lose an ingredient, shorten time).
5. Teams bid to sabotage competitors or protect themselves.
6. Begin the timer. Students must complete their task despite any obstacles. Encourage creative problem-solving, collaboration, and adaptability.

VARIATIONS

- Content customization
  - Culinary: Modify recipes or tools.
  - Design: Limit color palettes or materials.
  - Health science: Introduce new "patient" systems mid-procedure
  - Business/Marketing: Impose last-minute client changes or budget cuts.
- Randomly assign sabotage cards instead of using play money.
- Assign a new team leader mid-challenge.
- Use a random wheel or QR codes to reveal sabotages.
- Replace physical challenges with communication or teamwork-based sabotages (e.g., "silent round").

WHY THIS SUPPORTS MAGICAL LEARNING

- Students take responsibility for their decisions, navigate setbacks, and experience authentic consequences that build resilience and strategic thinking.
- Bidding, sabotages, and timed challenges create a sense of urgency and excitement, mirroring the pressure and competition found in real industry settings.
- Faced with unexpected obstacles, students must think critically, adapt quickly, and reimagine how to reach their goals, strengthening their inventive mindset.
- Teams communicate, experiment, and iterate together in fast-paced scenarios, learning to trust each other and grow from both success and failure.

Crime Scene Kitchen

Inspired by the hit reality series *Crime Scene Kitchen*, this immersive challenge blends mystery, strategy, and culinary skill. Students become "kitchen detectives," investigating clues to determine a mystery recipe before racing to re-create it. As they collaborate, analyze evidence, and problem-solve under pressure, they strengthen critical thinking, communication, and technical skills that apply across CTE pathways. This activity can be adapted for any content area by replacing the "recipe" with a concept, product, or process students must identify and create based on the clues provided.

TIME Ninety to 120 minutes (can be divided into two class periods)

MATERIALS

- Preselected mystery (or content-area task)
- Six to eight clues that point toward the correct answer
- Two or three false clues to challenge teams' reasoning
- Caution tape or props to stage a "crime scene" area
- Manila folders (optional, for contained visual clues)
- Digital note sheets for investigation notes
- Rubber gloves or costume props (optional, but fun!)
- Access to ingredients/tools (or materials relevant to subject)
- Music and visuals for atmosphere (optional)
- Timer

HOW TO PLAY

Phase one: The hook

1. Choose one of two ways to stage your clues:
    - Option one: Physical crime scene. Stage a table or kitchen station with six to eight clues that point to the recipe (e.g., used whisk, melted chocolate, lemon zest, etc.), along with a few red herrings. Cover with caution tape until reveal time.

- Option two: Evidence folder. Place photos or visual clues in a manila folder for each team.
2. Set the tone for mystery and excitement. As students enter, play dramatic theme music and display a "Crime Scene Kitchen" title screen. Optionally, wear a detective costume or lab coat and hand out rubber gloves.
3. Announce that a "culinary mystery" has been discovered and your students' mission is to solve it before time runs out.

Phase two: The crime scene investigation
4. Students are divided into teams of three to five and given three minutes to investigate. They must record every detail they observe, discuss what each clue might mean, and prepare questions for the next phase.

Phase three: Investigation and questioning
5. This phase builds reasoning and evidence-based communication skills. Teams have fifteen to thirty minutes to:
   - Collaborate and analyze their findings.
   - Research possible recipes (or concepts, depending on content).
   - Ask the "witness" (teacher) up to three yes/no questions based on their evidence.

Phase four: Mystery creation challenge
6. Teams use their best hypothesis to recreate or represent the mystery item. Students must demonstrate teamwork, time management, and technical accuracy as they work.
   - Culinary: Bake or prepare the dessert you believe matches the clues.
   - Design: Create the project prototype.
   - Health science: Demonstrate the correct medical procedure.
   - Business/marketing: Pitch the product concept.

Phase five: Judging and reflection
7. When time is up, teams present their creations. Judges (teacher, peers, or invited staff) evaluate accuracy, creativity, and teamwork.
8. Discussion questions:
    - What strategies helped your team interpret the clues?
    - How did you adapt when unsure of a hypothesis?
    - How does this relate to solving real-world problems in your field?

VARIATIONS
- Digital Version: Provide virtual "crime scenes" using images or slides. Students record evidence digitally.
- Career Pathway Adaptations:
    - Interior design: Solve clues that lead to a mystery room layout or design style.
    - Health science: Diagnose a "patient" based on symptom clues.
    - Child development: Match developmental milestones to "mystery child" profiles.
    - Business/marketing: Determine a mystery product from branding evidence.
    - Engineering/manufacturing: Identify a mystery mechanism or tool from materials and diagrams.
- Leadership rotation: Assign a different "lead detective" for each phase.

WHY THIS SUPPORTS MAGICAL LEARNING
- Students act as investigators, analyzing evidence, making informed decisions, and taking responsibility for their process from discovery to final creation.
- Time tasks, clue-based gameplay, and unfolding mysteries create an immersive experience that energizes learning and deepens skill development.
- Students interpret ambiguous information, connect ideas, and apply prior knowledge in inventive ways to uncover solutions.

- Through questioning, discussion, and teamwork, students communicate effectively and problem-solve together, turning curiosity into discovery.

Mystery Recipe Dash

If you are looking for a speedy way to bring in a little mystery to your cooking lab, you'll love this! I have used this version in my Amazing Race–International Cuisine and Amazing Food Truck–United States regional game plans to lead students to favorite regional specialties in the places we visit. However, it could be used in other areas of culinary as well, such as pies and pastries, soups and sauces, yeast breads, quick breads, etc. I would suggest students have some prior skill building in the recipe category before introducing this activity.

TIME Sixty to seventy-five minutes

MATERIALS
- Mystery Recipe
- Chromebook or other device
- Paper to record evidence
- Recipe ingredients
- Judging rubric/scorecard
- Timer

HOW TO PLAY
1. Select a recipe for each team of four or five students to prepare, eliminating the title.
2. Give students five minutes to read through the recipe and talk with their team to make sure they understand the recipe procedures.
3. Each team selects one team member to begin researching what the recipe title may be based on the ingredients and directions. The rest of the team will begin preparing the recipe once the time begins.

4. Set the timer for the amount of time you anticipate it will take your students to complete the recipe and send students to their kitchens to begin.
5. The researcher will stay behind to use their Chromebook or device to research. They will want to write down all the evidence they find on a piece of paper. After six minutes, shout out "switch" and another team member will trade places with the researcher and resume research and writing down evidence. The rotation through team members will continue throughout the challenge so all team members are able to help in the research and recipe preparation.
6. Once time is up, students will present their recipe creation to the judging panel and reveal their guess on the mystery title.
7. Judges will taste recipes for accuracy of taste, texture, and appearance and score each on a five-point scale. If the title of the recipe is guessed correctly, an additional ten points are given.

WHY THIS SUPPORTS MAGICAL LEARNING

* The unknown recipe and element of surprise immediately capture students' attention, turning anticipation into a memorable and engaging learning experience.
* By reading procedures, dividing roles, researching, and preparing a dish without knowing its name, students take responsibility for their learning and practice real-world problem solving under time constraints.
* Timed tasks, rotating research roles, and a scoring system infuse energy and competition, motivating students to stay focused and fully engaged throughout the experience.
* Students analyze clues, interpret recipes, and predict outcomes, strengthening their ability to think critically, adapt quickly, and perform in high-pressure environments.

Classic Game Shows Reimagined for the Classroom

Now that we've explored the power and potential of weaving reality competition elements into classroom learning, let's turn our attention to another genre that captures audiences in a different way: the classic game show. Before we dive in, let's differentiate between the two genres.

Reality competition shows, like *The Voice, Next Level Chef,* or *The Amazing Race*, are typically season-long stories broken into episodes that center around growth, storytelling, and transformation. Viewers become invested in the contestants' journeys over a period of time as they learn new skills, overcome obstacles, and evolve through mentorship and feedback. These shows invite authenticity and creativity, highlighting each contestant's unique voice and approach while emphasizing collaboration, reflection, and perseverance. When translated into the classroom experience, a season becomes a semester, and an episode becomes a class period. Just like show contestants are on a journey of growth and transformation, our students are as well.

Classic game shows, such as *The Price Is Right* or *Wheel of Fortune*, on the other hand, feature stand-alone episodes showcase knowledge and skills. They often incorporate chance and quick decision-making. Sometimes contestants are competing independently, and at other times they work collaboratively. The excitement comes from rapid-fire questions, spinning wheels, and the thrill of immediate success or loss. They're fun, fast-paced, and high-energy, but they focus on performance in the moment rather than personal growth over time.

In essence, reality competition shows celebrate the *process*, the story behind the success, while classic game shows celebrate the *product*, the quick win. Both can inspire classroom learning. While reality competition formats mirror the authentic, reflective, and iterative side of learning, classic game shows reflect the quick formative checks for understanding that help us gauge where students are in their learning and adapt as needed. In this section we will explore some of my favorite classic game show remixes that are fun and effective for formative assessment.

The Price Is Right Hi Lo Challenge

Inspired by the game show *The Price Is Right,* this activity brings strategy, estimation, and real-world budgeting skills into your classroom. Students compete to guess the price of items without going over. They also determine which are priced higher or lower than a baseline product. Originally designed for culinary arts, this challenge can easily be adapted to any CTE pathway to strengthen skills in financial literacy, critical thinking, and decision-making—essential in every career field.

TIME Forty-five to sixty minutes

MATERIALS
- Slide deck or digital display with images of six to eight items
- Accurate prices for each item (based on current market data)
- Recording sheets or whiteboards for answers
- Small prizes, badges, or incentives for winning team
- Play money, calculators, or digital scorecards (optional)

HOW TO PLAY
1. Select six items related to your current unit of study (ingredients, tools, materials, or supplies).
2. Assign accurate prices using local or online sources.
3. Choose one item to be the baseline item with a hidden price.
4. Create a slide deck with clear photos of each item, hiding the prices under each image.

OPTION ONE

1. Option Display all six items and tell students that one is the baseline item (e.g., "unsalted butter" or "power drill").
2. In teams, students decide which three of the remaining five items are priced higher than the baseline.
3. Once all teams lock in their answers, reveal the actual prices one at a time for added suspense.
4. Scoring:
   - All three correct: ten points
   - Two correct: eight points
   - One correct: five points
   - None correct: zero points (but still receive feedback)

OPTION TWO

1. Show one item at a time and have teams write down their best guess of the unit price (per pound, per dozen, per item, etc.).
2. A student spokesperson for each team guesses the price.
3. Closest guess without going over earns one point.
4. If all teams go over, no points are awarded.
5. Repeat for five to seven rounds, rotating the student spokesperson for each team.
6. Team with the most total points wins a classroom bonus (e.g., early lab access, first material pick. or badges).

VARIATIONS: BONUS TWIST (MYSTERY ROUND ITEM)

* Add an unexpected "mystery" or "premium" product for teams to debate and justify:
  - Culinary arts: saffron, truffle oil, or vanilla bean pods
  - Interior design: imported tile, designer fabric, or vintage light fixture
  - Health science: advanced diagnostic tool or specialty equipment
  - Business/marketing: advertising campaign budget item or luxury product

- ○ Manufacturing/engineering: high-grade metal, precision tool, or specialty component
* Teams must discuss why the item may be higher or lower in value and defend their reasoning before the reveal.

VARIATIONS: CTE PATHWAYS
* Culinary arts: Compare ingredient prices and food costs for recipe planning and menu design.
* Interior design: Estimate cost differences in materials like flooring, paint, and textiles.
* Fashion and apparel: Predict price differences between brands, materials, or production methods.
* Health science: Compare medical supply costs, equipment, or procedure fees.
* Business/marketing: Price consumer goods, advertisements, or packaging costs.
* Manufacturing/engineering: Estimate production costs or material expenses.
* Early childhood education: Compare prices of classroom supplies, toys, or curriculum materials.

WHY THIS SUPPORTS MAGICAL LEARNING
* Students make authentic decisions involving budgeting, cost analysis, and pricing connecting financial concepts directly to their chosen pathways.
* Competition, suspenseful reveals, and a dynamic point system transform learning into an interactive and motivating experience.
* Students use creative reasoning to justify pricing choices, evaluate outcomes, and reflect on the financial implications of their decisions.
* Teams discuss, debate, and problem-solve together as they explore the reasoning behind value, cost, and consumer perception.

Vocabulary Pyramid Challenge

In this activity inspired by the television game show *The $25,000 Pyramid*, students work in pairs to guess as many vocabulary terms as possible using short, descriptive clues tied to classroom content.

TIME Fifteen to twenty minutes

MATERIALS

* Physical or digital pyramid category board (template can be made in Canva, Slides, or printed)
* Vocabulary word cards for each category
* Whiteboards or notecards for scoring (optional)
* Timer

HOW TO PLAY

1. Create six pyramid-style categories based on your current unit.
   - Culinary arts: kitchen equipment, cooking methods, sanitation, and safety
   - Business/marketing: advertising strategies, financial terms, customer service
   - Health science: anatomy, medical procedures, patient care tools
   - Design: color theory, sewing terms, design principles
   - Early childhood education: developmental stages, learning styles, classroom tools
2. Under each category, list five to seven vocabulary terms.
3. Pair up students: One student is the clue-giver, and the other is the guesser.
4. Display the pyramid game board.

5. Have teams pick a category at random (or use a digital spinner for added suspense).
6. Each team takes turns competing while others observe and cheer them on.
7. The clue-giver describes each word without using the word (or its root), spelling it, or rhyming. The guesser calls out their answers within the sixty-second time limit.
8. Each correct guess equals one point. A bonus point is awarded to a team who guesses all words in a category.
9. After the game, use reflection prompts to discuss the learning:
    - What strategies helped you communicate clues effectively?
    - Which words were the hardest to guess and why?
    - How could you use this vocabulary in your next lab, project, or presentation?

VARIATIONS

✳ Tournament style: Winners from each round go head-to-head in a final championship round. Use a lightning round with only thirty seconds per round and more advanced vocabulary.

✳ Rotation style: Rotate partners after each round so students practice clue-giving and guessing with new peers, increasing communication and collaboration.

✳ Wild card challenge: Add a mystery envelope that includes a bonus challenge like:
    - Act out one of the vocabulary words.
    - Draw the word instead of describing it.
    - Use only *three* total words to describe each item in a round.

WHY THIS SUPPORTS MAGICAL LEARNING

✳ Students take ownership of their learning as they explain and interpret key concepts in their own words, developing professional communication and content mastery.

* Encourages creative ways to communicate meaning. Students must think on their feet, use descriptive language, and innovate how they convey ideas.
* The back-and-forth clue-giving and guessing build collaboration, curiosity, and quick problem-solving under pressure.
* Strengthens students' confidence in subject-specific language and their ability to think and communicate effectively—skills that transfer to every career pathway.

Skill Showdown

In this challenge inspired by television game show *Minute to Win It*, students race against the clock to complete short, skill-based challenges that reinforce course competencies—all in under sixty seconds.

TIME Ten to twenty-five minutes (adaptable)

MATERIALS
* Varies by challenge. Keep it simple and subject-relevant.

HOW TO PLAY
1. Choose your format:
    - Station rotation: Set up several timed skill stations around the room.
    - Team relay: Each team member completes one skill challenge before tagging in the next.
    - Class showdown: All students complete the same task one at a time, tournament-style.
2. Set a timer for sixty seconds and project it on the screen or use a dramatic countdown sound effect.
3. Challenges can vary based on CTE pathways:
    - Culinary arts: Crack and separate an egg (no yolk breakage!); accurately measure flour, sugar, and liquid into labeled containers;

set a formal place setting from memory; or whisk cream until soft peaks form.
    - Child development: Diaper and dress a baby doll using appropriate steps; sort toys by age-appropriateness; or stack blocks to a specified height using only one hand.
    - Construction/engineering: Hammer five nails into a soft board (predrilled if needed); assemble a structure using LEGO or wood parts; properly use and name three hand tools.
    - Personal finance: Categorize ten expenses into fixed/variable in under a minute; match budget items to their definitions; build a budget with cash envelopes labeled for groceries, rent, savings, etc.
4. Scoring
    - Pass/fail: Pass equals one point, fail equals zero.
    - Timed accuracy: Add bonus points for speed and precision.
    - Style points: Bonus for creativity, teamwork, or flair (as determined by the teacher or peer judges).
5. Use prompts to reflect after the game:
    - What strategy helped you complete the challenge quickly?
    - If you could redo this task, what would you change?
    - How could this skill be applied in a real-life scenario?

VARIATIONS

- Bell-ringer boost: Start class with a single sixty-second challenge related to the day's objective. Fast, focused, and fun.
- Skill surge showdown: Use as a review or end-of-unit celebration. Teams rotate through multiple skill stations, earning points for each completed task.
- Random challenge generator: Write challenge names on slips of paper or use a digital spinner (like wheelofnames.com) to randomly assign tasks to teams or students.

* Mystery box challenge: Place materials for a skill challenge in a mystery bag or box. Students open it, read the challenge card, and complete it on the spot.

WHY THIS SUPPORTS MAGICAL LEARNING

* Students apply real-world skills under pressure, simulating the fast-paced decision-making and precision often required in professional environments. Each learner takes ownership of their performance and technique.
* Students must think on their feet and find creative, efficient ways to complete the task within the time limit, encouraging adaptability and problem-solving.
* The sixty-second time limit, point system, and competitive atmosphere transform traditional practice into a fast-paced game-like experience that motivates participation and persistence.

Guess the Term

Inspired by the television game show *Wheel of Fortune*, Guess the Term is a fast-paced, team-based vocabulary challenge where students reveal letters to uncover unit-based terms or phrases. Each spin of the wheel adds suspense and strategy as teams collaborate to solve the puzzle before their competitors. This activity reinforces academic vocabulary, communication, teamwork, and critical thinking, while offering a fun, gamified way to review and apply key concepts across all CTE pathways.

TIME Thirty to forty minutes

MATERIALS

* Digital wheel spinner
* Word or phrase puzzles (use a whiteboard, slideshow, or digital game board)
* Dry-erase board or slide deck for scoreboard

- Mini challenge cards (optional for bonus challenges)
- Timer

HOW TO PLAY

1. Divide the class into two to four teams (depending on class size). Each team should select a spokesperson.
2. Display a puzzle with blank spaces representing one letter in the term or phrase of the solution.
3. The first team spins the wheel to determine their point value.
4. The team guesses a consonant. If that letter appears in the solution, fill in the matching spaces and award the points multiplied by the number of times the letter appears. If the guess as incorrect, play passes to the next team.
5. Teams can buy a vowel for points.
6. Teams can attempt to solve the full term or phrase on their turn after any correct guess.
7. A correct solution earns bonus points. An incorrect guess ends their turn and forfeits that round's points.
8. Use prompts to reflect after the game: What strategies helped your team solve puzzles quickly and accurately? Which vocabulary terms challenged you most, and why? How could you apply these terms or concepts in your next lab, project, or real-world scenario?

VARIATION: BONUS CHALLENGES

- After solving, the winning team gets a mini challenge card to deepen leaning:
    - Define the term in your own words.
    - Provide a real-world example from your CTE area.
    - Demonstrate or describe the skill associated with the term.

CLASSROOM APPLICATION IDEAS

* Family and science / culinary arts: "mise en place," "cross contamination," "rolling boil," "braising," "mother sauces" "define this term," "give a kitchen example," or "show the technique."
* Child development: "fine motor skills," "positive reinforcement," "attachment theory"
* Interior design: "color harmony," "feng shui," "open floor plan"
* Personal finance: "compound interest," "financial literacy," "fixed expenses"
* Entrepreneurship: "target audience," "profit margin," "marketing mix"

GAME VARIATIONS

* Lightning round: Teams have thirty seconds to solve rapid-fire puzzles worth double points.
* Mystery wheel: Include "bonus spaces" (e.g., five points, skip next team, switch letters).
* Team relay: After solving the puzzle, the team must complete a related minitask (e.g., label a diagram, identify a tool, or list safety steps).
* Digital version: Use platforms like Google Slides, Flippity, or Genially for interactive puzzles and automatic scoring.

WHY HIS SUPPORTS MAGICAL LEARNING

* Students take the lead as clue-solvers and content experts, building confidence through active participation and mastery of professional vocabulary.
* Encourages creative reasoning and deductive thinking as students connect clues, analyze word structure, and apply contextual knowledge
* Teams communicate, debate, and collaborate to uncover each term, fueling curiosity about how vocabulary connects to real-world skills.
* The point system, wheel spins, and bonus challenges add layers of strategy, motivation, and fun that make learning feel like play.

PERMISSION TO BINGE-WATCH!

There are hundreds of games just waiting to be adapted from television game shows, and you officially have permission to binge-watch for inspiration! Trust me, the more you watch, the more your mind will start to swirl with creative possibilities.

Don't overthink it! Lean into memorable beginnings by bringing the energy, anticipation, and excitement from your favorite shows into your classroom. When inspiration strikes, be fearless and give it a go. If it flops, tweak it and try again. I've learned that my students value authenticity and creativity, even when things don't go perfectly. In fact, those imperfect moments often spark collaboration and innovation, especially when I invite students to help refine and improve the experience. When learners have agency in shaping the fun, the results are always more magical than anything I could design alone.

So the next time you have the remote and a free evening, flip through some game shows, take notes on what makes them engaging, and let your curiosity and imagination run wild! You never know what classroom magic might be waiting to unfold!

CHAPTER 7

AI as a Creative Partner for Gamified Learning

USING AI TO SPARK IDEAS FOR GAMES AND LEARNING EXPERIENCES

Most days I leave school utterly exhausted. I am starving, my feet hurt, and I don't want to talk. Teaching career and technical education is amazingly rewarding, but it's nonstop. There are many days when I don't ever sit down. Let's face it, sometimes your brain is too full (or too fried) to brainstorm new games or learning hooks.

Luckily, AI is here to help. AI tools can help teachers create custom games, storytelling scenarios, and clue-based activities that spark curiosity, build confidence, and deepen learning in less than half the time it would take to use conventional methods.

For those of you who might worry that AI will replace your creativity, I have actually found the reverse to be true. Rather than replacing my creativity, I have found that AI has sparked new ways of approaching learning and expanded my creativity in ways I had never considered. As I'll lay out in this chapter, when used with intention, AI can actually remove roadblocks and save you time so you can spend your energy crafting memorable, meaningful, and joyful learning experiences your students will love. AI takes care of the mundane, so you can focus on the joy.

GENERATING PROMPTS THAT GET RESULTS

In CTE, our content is naturally rich with real-world problems, and there are infinite challenge activities we can present to our students. With AI as a thinking partner, you can generate dozens of challenge ideas in minutes and customize them for your content, students, and classroom vibe. I can't begin to tell you how much collaborating with AI large language models (LLMs) such as ChatGPT, Claude, and Gemini has sparked my creativity and provided ideas that I've been able to develop to create incredible experiences for my students.

But responses from LLMs are only going to be as good as the input you provide. Rather than making vague requests such as:

* "Give me five gamified review activities for a high school culinary arts class studying food safety."
* "Design a classroom game using interior design vocabulary and a spinner."
* "Create a team challenge for child development students to explore positive guidance strategies."

Consider refining your prompts to include more clarity and detail:

* "Design five engaging, gamified review activities for a high school culinary arts class studying food safety. Each activity should be interactive, promote student collaboration, and reinforce key concepts related to food safety (e.g., proper handling, cooking temperatures, cross contamination, hygiene). Provide a brief description of how each game works, materials needed, and how it ties back to the learning objectives."
* "Create a classroom game for high school interior design students that utilizes key vocabulary terms. Incorporate a spinner

as the main game mechanic. The game should promote critical thinking, teamwork, and allow students to demonstrate their understanding of interior design concepts. Provide instructions, how the spinner works, and a list of potential vocabulary terms to include."

✳ "Design a team challenge for child development students focused on exploring positive guidance strategies. The challenge should encourage problem-solving, teamwork, and creativity while reinforcing concepts such as positive reinforcement, setting limits, and encouraging independence. Include the structure of the challenge, the specific roles of team members, and how students will present their strategies."

So how can you transform your prompts from bland to brilliant? There are many amazing resources being developed for prompt engineering, and I am by no means an expert. However, as I've done my own research and honed my prompt engineering skills, I've created an acronym that provides me guidelines to consider as I am collaborating with generative AI. You will not be surprised that it spells out MAGIC! Ha! In the below image I break down the guidelines as well as an example prompt.

 Make the objective clear

Purpose: Ensures the AI understands the goal of the task.

How it works: When you clearly state the *desired outcome* (i.e., what you want students to learn or achieve), the AI can generate responses that align with your teaching goals.

Example: "Design a hands-on activity to teach high school students about food safety practices." This clarifies that the focus is on teaching food safety and that you want an experiential learning activity.

Add context and constraints

Purpose: Provides important background or limits to guide the response.

How it works: Context (like grade level or subject) and constraints (such as time, resources, or budget) narrow down the response, making it more practical and relevant.

Example: "Create a team challenge for high school students studying child development, focusing on positive guidance strategies, within a thirty-minute class period." This gives the AI context (child development and guidance strategies) and a constraint (time limit), so the response fits your classroom needs.

 ### Give a teaching style or method

Purpose: Directs the AI to tailor its response to a specific instructional approach.

How it works: You can specify the type of learning activity (e.g., game-based learning, project-based learning, inquiry-based learning) to match your preferred teaching style.

Example: "Design a collaborative project for culinary students that encourages critical thinking and teamwork." This specifies that the activity should involve collaboration and critical thinking, aligning with a project-based teaching style.

Indicate specific outputs needed

Purpose: Ensures that the AI provides exactly what you need (e.g., a game, a lesson plan, an activity).

How it works: When you state what format or type of output you need (list, activity, rubric), the AI will deliver something actionable and ready to implement.

Example: "Create a rubric to assess high school students' safety practices during a lab activity." This specifies the need for a rubric, giving the AI clear direction on the output format.

Clarify and iterate

Purpose: Helps refine and improve the response to meet your exact needs.

How it works: If the first response isn't perfect, provide clarification or feedback, asking the AI to make revisions or adjust the solution. Iteration ensures you get exactly what you're looking for.

Example: "Revise the classroom activity you suggested, but make it more interactive and include materials students can work with in pairs." This clarifies that you want a more interactive version and provides additional details to guide the revision.

As your LLM of choice gets to know you through your conversations, the responses are going to be more and more tailored to you and your teaching style. Viewing AI as a thought partner has saved me unmeasurable amounts of time. Now I can create even more amazing experiences for my students because I have more time to create and plan!

While communicating with LLMs, it is important to keep your information safe. Avoid sharing personal identifiable information, confidential or sensitive information, and detailed context or specific scenarios that could potentially identify individuals. The goal is to leverage the power of AI while maintaining responsible, safe communication practices.

AI AS YOUR CREATIVE GAME DESIGN PARTNER

The first time I encountered Breakout EDU was on a converted school bus at the International Society for Technology in Education (ISTE) conference in Denver, Colorado. As I entered the bus, I was transported into an immersive storyline with clues to solve and locks to break open within a designated timeframe. The experience stuck with me, but truthfully, I felt intimidated by the idea of running one myself. Locks? Codes? Would I even be able to set it up, let alone create one from scratch?

Then my friend Ann Brucker, a game designer from Breakout EDU, created a custom game for my book *Make Learning MAGICAL* and facilitated it at a local teacher summit. Watching her guide teachers through clues, locks, and collaboration gave me the confidence to give it a try. Soon, I was designing games, setting locks, and watching students light up as they pieced together clues and cracked the code.

One moment stands out. A fifth-grade student blurted out mid-game, "You guys! We have to be smarter than we normally are if we're going to figure this out!" That same day, a struggling learner said, "This was the first time I didn't give up." Why? Because curiosity fueled engagement. Play made learning irresistible.

That experience was a turning point.

I began to think about how we could embed that feeling of curiosity into the flow of learning, not just for one day, but across an entire unit. That's when I had an idea inspired by the popular reality competition show *The Masked Singer*. What if we designed our units like a season of a show, unfolding clues over time to culminate in a big reveal? Each week, students would gather hints, solve puzzles, and decode content-related clues that eventually unlocked a Breakout EDU box (or digital equivalent). Inside could be a badge, a challenge, a reward, or simply the satisfaction of solving the mystery together.

Though this idea was exciting to think about, it takes time and creative energy to implement. And I'm sure I'm not alone in feeling like there is never enough of either commodity. Sometimes our best ideas lay dormant because we don't have the energy or minutes in the day available to turn them into a reality. But now, thanks to timesaving AI tools, creating these immersive experiences is more accessible than ever.

Whether you're designing physical escape rooms or digital breakout challenges, AI can:

* Generate clues (riddles, rhymes, rebus puzzles, emoji codes) tied directly to your unit content
* Design lock combinations (four-digit, directional, letter, or shape-based) based on your subject matter
* Build logic puzzles and trivia tasks that reinforce key concepts
* Create scavenger hunts with QR codes, visual cues, or hidden text
* Write compelling narratives to frame your escape room in a story-based context

Let's say you're teaching a unit on world cuisines in a culinary class. AI can help you:

* Create a "Top Secret Recipe" mystery box where students unlock clues based on flavor profiles or historical food origins
* Generate riddles that lead to a specific Michelin-starred restaurant
* Build a story around a missing chef's journal that guides students to follow kitchen "evidence" to retrieve it before time runs out

In my culinary arts 3 class, I created a Midwestern cuisine escape room. I used AI to generate clues based on regional dishes and cultural influences. This included clues that led students to codes that unlocked a directional lock, five-digit number lock, a letter lock, and a shape lock. The result? Students collaborated deeply, laughed often, and never once asked, "Is this on the test?"

AI doesn't replace your creativity, it enhances it. It helps you build faster, think bigger, and focus on the experience rather than starting from scratch every time.

Whether it's a mystery box or a masked singer, curiosity is the hook that pulls us in. When we tap into that drive to discover, solve, and unlock, we engage students in deep learning without it ever feeling like a chore. And with AI in your corner, you don't have to be a full-time puzzle master to create unforgettable experiences. So go ahead. Let your classroom feel a little more like a game show or mystery novel. Hand your students the magnifying glass, or the combination lock, and let curiosity lead the way.

AI-POWERED STORYTELLING AND PERSONALIZED CHALLENGES

Gamified learning is at its best when there's a story. A powerful narrative transforms a simple activity into an immersive adventure by giving purpose to the challenge, context to the content, and emotion to the experience. Stories invite students to step into roles, make choices, and care about the outcome. But crafting those storylines, missions, clues, character arcs, and plot twists that make learning come alive can be incredibly time-consuming, especially when balancing lesson planning, grading, and everything else on an educator's plate. Developing the right tone, dialogue, and pacing often takes hours that teachers simply don't have. That's where AI becomes a game-changer. With a few thoughtful prompts, you can brainstorm story ideas, generate character descriptions, or build a full narrative framework in minutes. AI helps you move from idea to memorable beginning faster, freeing you to focus on the creative touches that make the experience truly magical.

Try using AI to:

- ✳ Create client scenarios for interior design or culinary projects
- ✳ Write background stories for mystery boxes or escape room experiences

- Generate quests or missions for students to "level up"
- Personalize role cards or challenge descriptions using student input

Here's a classroom example: For a child development class, you can use AI to generate realistic scenarios centered around common parenting dilemmas such as bedtime struggles, screen-time battles, or sibling conflicts. When prompting AI, be specific and ask it to scaffold the stories from simple to complex or align them with your course standards and competencies. You can also request representation across diverse family structures, cultures, and parenting contexts to ensure inclusivity and authenticity. Once you have partnered with AI to create the scenarios, design an activity where students work in teams to analyze each situation, discuss possible responses, and select a course of action that balances empathy, discipline, and developmental appropriateness. Continue the collaboration by asking AI to help you craft debrief prompts such as "What would you do differently?" or "Which parenting philosophy best aligns with your response?" to encourage meaningful reflection and discussion.

AI GAME DESIGN PROMPT GUIDE FOR CTE TEACHERS

If you are still feeling a bit intimidated or unsure of how to use AI, don't worry—I've got you! I have created some scaffolding below to assist you in communicating with AI. Using the MAGIC prompt guidelines, customize these prompt starters below to spark creativity and build gamified experiences in your CTE classroom. Remember, the more details and context you give it, the better the responses will be!

General Prompts

- "Create a classroom game to review key concepts in [CTE subject]."

- "Design a simulation for students to practice [skill]."
- "Give me five vocabulary-based games for high school [subject] class."
- "Write a story-based challenge for students learning [topic]."
- "Generate clues for a four-digit lock using facts about [unit topic]."

Culinary Arts

- "Create an *Amazing Race*-style culinary challenge reviewing kitchen safety."
- "Write a story for a mystery recipe challenge that uses AI-generated clues."
- "Design a food truck pitch game with scoring criteria for creativity and cost-efficiency."

Child Development

- "Generate fictional toddler profiles with development needs and behavior scenarios."
- "Design a simulation where students plan a preschool activity based on a child's profile."
- "Create a role-play challenge focused on positive guidance strategies."

Interior Design

- "Build a team challenge where students design themed dorm rooms with client feedback twists."
- "Create a simulation with fictional clients requesting sustainable design elements."
- "Generate a four-pic, one-word puzzle using design elements or terms."

Personal Finance

* "Create a budgeting simulation with life-event cards that affect income and expenses."
* "Write a *Shark Tank*–style pitch where students defend their monthly budget plan."
* "Design a game where students compete to reach financial goals using choice cards."

Fashion/Clothing

* "Design a runway challenge using constraints like fabric type or client need."
* "Generate client profiles for tailoring or styling scenarios."
* "Create a digital scavenger hunt using fashion terms."

BEFORE VS. WITH AI: PLANNING TIME AND IMPACT

I have found that the more collaboratively I work with AI as a thought partner, the more time I save. To better illustrate my point, I have compared the time it takes me to create tasks or activities with and without AI assistance.

Before AI, designing creative, game-based learning experiences could take hours. Building a vocabulary review game might require one to two hours of brainstorming and formatting, while writing a collaborative clue-based escape room with multiple locks could stretch into two or three. Developing character-driven client scenarios often took nearly an hour, and mapping out a full unit challenge complete with story and game flow could consume an entire afternoon or more. Even creating printable game cards or boards might take an hour of design work on its own.

With AI, those same tasks can happen in a fraction of the time. A vocabulary-based review game can take just ten to fifteen minutes to generate. A full escape room outline, once an afternoon's work, can be written in twenty to thirty minutes. Client scenarios appear in minutes, and a complete unit challenge with narrative and structure can be built in under an hour. Even visualizing printable cards or boards now takes only about ten minutes with Canva and AI working together.

The bottom line is this: AI doesn't replace your creativity; it removes the roadblocks that slow it down. By using AI as a thought partner, you will have more time to act on your creative ideas and make them a reality. And the more your students become empowered learners, the more motivation and excitement you will have to create meaningful and joyful learning experiences for students.

THE FUTURE OF AI IN GAMIFIED LEARNING

We're only beginning to understand what AI can do in CTE classrooms. As the tools grow more dynamic, we'll be able to co-create even more powerful learning experiences, like:

- Adaptive learning paths where the next challenge is based on student choices
- Real-time roleplay with AI-powered clients
- Dynamic storytelling games that change as students play
- AI-assisted portfolio feedback or digital rubrics
- Voice-generated audio clues, custom rubrics, or scenario narration

AI won't replace teachers. But it *will* help us design faster, plan better, and imagine more boldly.

CHAPTER 8

Creating an Inclusive and Joyful CTE Classroom

BRINGING THE DRAGON SMART PHILOSOPHY TO LIFE IN YOUR TEACHING

As an educator, parent, and passionate advocate for kids, I've always believed in the magic every child brings into this world. But sometimes, the traditional markers of success don't tell the whole story. This realization hit close to home as I watched my son, Tommy, navigate school.

Tommy is one of the most dedicated learners I know. He listens, studies, and puts his heart into everything he does. Yet no matter how hard he worked, school often felt like an impossible maze. Words didn't always line up, numbers blurred, and standardized tests never quite captured the brilliance I saw every day. I'm sure many of you reading this can vividly picture a child like Tommy: someone who pours their soul into learning yet remains unseen by systems prioritizing a narrow definition of success.

But here's the thing about Tommy: His creativity is boundless, and his ability to bring ideas to life is breathtaking. Watching him find his voice through art was a powerful reminder that intelligence isn't one-size-fits-all. This realization became the heartbeat of the children's book Tommy and I created together, *Dragon Smart*, which tells a story that celebrates every child's unique strengths and reminds us all that intelligence is beautifully diverse.

Throughout my three decades in education, first as a teacher then as a technology integration specialist and now again in the culinary arts classroom, I've encountered many students who, like Tommy, don't fit the conventional school mold. Often labeled as struggling or distracted, these neurodivergent learners possess remarkable strengths that traditional assessments frequently overlook. Because of the experiential nature of our CTE classrooms, we have the perfect landscape to empower a diverse array of learners.

This chapter is about making small but powerful shifts that transform our classrooms into magical learning spaces where every student, whether they're a dreamer, problem-solver, builder, or creator, can fully engage, thrive, and shine. Together, we will explore how to design authentic and inclusive environments where every child feels seen, supported, and valued, and where diverse intelligences are not only recognized but celebrated. When we lead with memorable beginnings, spark creativity and curiosity, and give students agency to take ownership of their learning, we create classrooms filled with joy, purpose, and possibility. When we shift our focus from what students cannot do to what they can, we unlock the legacy of learning, and a lasting sense of confidence, connection, and wonder stays with them long after they leave our classrooms.

UNDERSTANDING NEURODIVERGENT LEARNERS IN CTE

One of my favorite lab demonstrations every semester is how to make fresh pasta. One class period while I was demonstrating, a boy (I'll call him Marcus) appeared to be unfocused, distracted, and unengaged. Instead of looking at what I was demonstrating, he was fidgeting with a measuring cup on the stainless steel table in front of him. I was annoyed that he wasn't paying attention, and I was already anticipating having to repeat what I had shown the class. However, when it came time to cook, Marcus not only recalled every step, but also improvised the sauce's herb blend with a surprisingly delicious result. Though he appeared to be not paying attention, he actually was. His mind was processing information differently—and powerfully. This is often the case with neurodivergent learners like those with ADHD, autism, or dyslexia: they learn in unique ways that standard classrooms may overlook, yet these differences can become tremendous strengths in a CTE setting.

Research supports what Marcus, and many others, have taught me through the years. Students with ADHD, for example, tend to excel in divergent thinking. They have the ability to generate many creative ideas from a single starting point.[11] In other words, the very "wandering mind" that gets them in trouble during lectures can fuel innovation and problem-solving. Likewise, autistic learners might have exceptional visual processing and pattern-recognition abilities.[12] I once had a student with autism who had an incredible ability to precisely cut vegetables with perfect consistency. Every dice and batonnet was exactly uniform, something seasoned chefs would envy. Her exceptional attention to detail not only made dishes visually appealing but also meant the ingredients cooked evenly, showcasing her unique strength beautifully. Dyslexic learners, known for struggling with reading, often show remarkable visual-spatial skills and out-of-the-box thinking.[13] A dyslexic student in my culinary class who struggled reading recipes could perfectly visualize plating presentations in her mind. Her dishes were like edible art. These examples echo a larger truth: neurodivergent students' brains are not deficient; they simply process

---

11 Holly White, "The Creativity of ADHD," *Scientific American*, February 20, 2024, https://www.scientificamerican.com/article/the-creativity-of-adhd/.

12 Amanda Chan, "Autistic Brain Excels at Recognizing Patterns," *LiveScience*, May 30, 2013, https://www.livescience.com/35586-autism-brain-activity-regions-perception.html.

13 Megan Anna Neff, "The Upside of Dyslexia: Exploring 5 Hidden Strengths," Neurodivergent Insights, accessed July 5, 2025 https://neurodivergentinsights.com/blog/dyslexia-strengths.

information differently. Often, areas where they experience challenges exist right alongside extraordinary strengths and talents, highlighting their unique and powerful ways of learning. Our job as CTE educators is to recognize and nurture those strengths.

Over the years, I've had countless culinary classes that have deepened my understanding of neurodiversity. However, I am not claiming to be an expert. I am still learning and will continue to learn so that I can provide the best learning experiences possible for my students. Time and time again, I've watched students shine in unexpected ways when given space to work collaboratively and play to their strengths. I've seen students who struggle with verbal communication become the most organized timekeepers and planners, creating step-by-step visuals or checklists for their teams. I've watched others, bursting with energy and ideas, take on the role of flavor innovators, bringing fearless creativity to every dish. These experiences have shown me that when we embrace different ways of thinking, our classrooms and our classroom labs become places where every student can thrive and neurodivergent processing differences can be powerful assets. In fact, recognizing these strengths is a key principle of the Dragon Smart philosophy. Just as the character Tommy the Dragon discovers his brilliance in creativity and a kind heart despite struggling in school, our neurodivergent students often reveal gifts that shine when given the right environment. By understanding how they learn, whether it's through movement, visuals, hyperfocus on a passion, or storytelling, we can design CTE experiences that let them thrive. And in doing so, we validate the message that intelligence is not one-size-fits-all. Every learner has their own form of "dragon magic" waiting to be unleashed.

BUILDING A TRULY INCLUSIVE CTE CLASSROOM

Think about a student's first impression when walking into your classroom. Does the environment quietly say, "You belong here, and you can thrive here"? Building a truly inclusive classroom starts with that sense of belonging and continues with every routine and practice that unfolds daily. When I began teaching in my culinary classroom, I began by reexamining the physical setup. I noticed that some of my students were uncomfortable or anxious with the table arrangement. We had too many tables and not enough space to walk between them. There were also many additional items that made it feel closed in. I realized that not all of the tables were needed to seat everyone comfortably, so we removed three of them and spaced them further apart. I also removed things that weren't necessary and tried to create a calming space for students. By making these changes I could feel the reduced anxiety from students who struggled with sensory overload. The positive effects were tangible.

In a CTE classroom, flexibility can look different depending on the learning environment. In a culinary lab, a student who struggles to sit still during demonstrations might benefit from helping with ingredient setup at a standing prep station, allowing them to stay engaged while moving. In an interior design or fashion lab, providing options like drafting tables, swivel stools, or floor seating with clipboards can help students choose how they focus best during sketching or pattern work. In a health science or early childhood classroom, offering both quiet reflection zones for journaling and collaborative tables for group simulations supports students who need calm spaces to process or movement to think. Even in a construction or engineering shop, giving learners the choice to observe a demonstration from a standing workstation or seated bench honors different sensory and focus needs.

A flexible learning environment that includes these choices helps each student learn in a way that works best for them. You could establish different zones: a traditional table for written work, a stand-up or bistro table for those who focus better on their feet, and a quiet corner with a stool and noise-canceling headphones for anyone needing a sensory break. Instead of rigid seating charts, offer students choice in where to work depending on the activity.

These small adjustments can be transformational. The student who once asked to go to the restroom every ten minutes to move their body might now transition to the bistro table to stand and continue working productively. In a lab, a student who struggles with overstimulation can choose a quieter corner to focus. These shifts signal to neurodivergent learners that their needs are not an inconvenience but a valued part of classroom design. When students see that flexibility and belonging are built into the environment, they are more likely to engage, regulate, and thrive.

Beyond furniture and space, predictable routines and visual supports are the backbone of an inclusive CTE classroom. As I discussed in chapter 3, routines are essential to building trust and a sense of community for all students in the classroom—and they're particularly useful for neurodivergent students. At the start of each class, I project a simple visual overview that shows the main focus of the lesson and picture, the lesson objectives (plan), and anything I want them to begin as I'm taking attendance. This kind of visual overview helps students with autism or anxiety know what to expect, reducing the worry about what's coming next. There have been a few times this year, for one reason or another, that I didn't have the overview on the projector when students walked in. The change in atmosphere was palpable. I could tell immediately that they relied on the predictable visual to help them feel grounded and secure in the plan for the day.

There is a pattern to my daily schedule as well. A typical class period for me goes as follows:

- First five minutes: Students transition as I take roll. This may include picking up necessary papers and reading through the recipe for the day or playing a game to review terminology.
- Ten minutes: Demonstration and instruction for the day's lab.
- Forty minutes: Lab experience.
- Fifteen minutes: Cleanup and reflection.

I am also intentional about providing adequate transitional clues for students. In my classroom, that involves giving verbal cues when we need to transition so students aren't caught off guard. For example, I may call out the time and let them know at what time they should be at a certain point in the recipe to keep on track. This helps students pace themselves and helps avoid a dismissal bell catching them by surprise and creating panic.

That doesn't mean I can never change up this routine. Sometimes, throwing a curve ball to add an element of surprise is fun. When change does happen, we frame it as another learning experience (sometimes we deliberately "flip" a routine to practice flexibility, discussing it openly). However, I have found that creating a predictable rhythm and flow helps reduce anxiety and provides a sense of security for students with autism. It actually benefits everyone for students to have a routine they can rely on.

Inclusivity also means rethinking how we present information and how students engage with content. In a culinary arts lesson, for example, I might have traditionally assigned a chapter reading on safety and sanitation with corresponding chapter questions or a worksheet. Now, I provide multiple options for students to show what they know. I may give them the choice of either creating an infographic, video, or comic strip to demonstrate their understanding instead of chapter questions or a worksheet. This aligns with the Universal Design for Learning principle of offering varied ways to access content and express knowledge.[14] A student with dyslexia can opt for the video or infographic and not be left behind, while another who loves reading can dive into the text.

In the culinary lab, I started teaching students how to sketchnote the steps of a recipe (aka "sketchipes") during my demonstrations. This form of visual note-taking helps students break down a complex

---

14 Rachael Radick, "Designing In-Person Training for All: Embracing Neurodiversity in the Classroom," *Education Northwest*, November 2024, https://educationnorthwest.org/insights/designing-person-training-all-embracing-neurodiversity-classroom.

cooking task into step-by-step pictures and simple words. My students who struggled with big blocks of text followed these visual cues with confidence. Visual supports like this are *not* just gimmicks; they're proven to help neurodivergent students comprehend and retain information more effectively.[15] As a bonus, they help avoid missteps in a busy kitchen environment with lots of distractions.

Let's not forget sensory and social support as part of inclusion. The loud noises, strong smells, and movement of a CTE classroom can be overwhelming. The loud and abrasive sound of power tools and equipment and team chatter, the sharp and pungent smell of food or chemicals, the heat from ovens and welders, the sparks or bright lights. All of these are examples of how overstimulating our CTE classes can be for students. I allow anyone who feels overstimulated or anxious to step outside the lab for a two-minute reset without penalty. Just knowing that escape exists has prevented panic in some students. For group work, I intentionally teach and model teamwork skills, because some neurodivergent learners may not intuitively pick up on social cues. We discuss what effective communication looks like in a kitchen team, and I assign rotating roles (executive chef, sous chef, prep cook, sanitation manager) to structure interactions. This kind of scaffolded social structure helps students with autism or ADHD practice collaboration in a clear, supported way.

Inclusion is not a one-time checklist; it's an ongoing mindset. I continually seek student input. Are the lights too bright? Should we play background music during labs or is that distracting? One year, I implemented a "question jar" where students could write anonymous questions if they were too shy or processing-delayed to ask in person. I have also posted a QR code that leads to a Google Form where students could add their questions as well. This was a hit, as it gave a voice to those who need more time to formulate thoughts. By building

---

15 Whitney Loring and Mary Hamilton, "Visual Supports and Autism Spectrum Disorders," Autism Speaks Autism Treatment Network, Vanderbilt University Medical Center, https://vkc.vumc.org/vkc/resources/autism/.

flexibility into the environment, routine into the schedule, and choice into learning, we create a classroom where all learners feel supported. And when students feel safe and understood, they blossom. In such a space, neurodivergent kids are more willing to take risks and share their talents. The inclusive CTE classroom, much like a well-run kitchen, thrives on the diversity of ingredients, people, and ideas. Our role as teachers is to stir all those unique flavors together into a harmonious—and delicious—learning experience.

INFUSING JOY AND CREATIVITY TO SUPPORT THE NEURODIVERGENT LEARNER

As we've explored throughout this book, joy is a powerful catalyst in any classroom, but it can be especially transformative for neurodivergent students. When students experience joy, their brains release dopamine and endorphins that enhance focus, memory, and motivation. Engaging, creative experiences such as Cupcake Wars and Mystery Box Challenges offer a playful outlet for exploration, innovation, and connection. For many neurodivergent learners, much of the school day is spent managing sensory input or masking differences to fit in. By intentionally creating moments of joy, we offer emotional safety, reduce anxiety, and open the door for authentic learning to flourish.

This past week, my culinary classes prepared cupcakes and cookies for prom. I could have provided them with the exact color palette and design plan to compliment the theme. However, allowing students to take ownership of the catering assignment created buy-in from the students and empowered them in ways that wouldn't have been possible if I hadn't allowed them some agency in the choices. All students, regardless of neurotype, were empowered to take risks, collaborate, and experience the satisfaction of success on their own terms. The kitchen positively buzzed with excitement. A neurodivergent student, who struggles with attention, hyperfocused for a solid hour as he experimented with mixing colors to fit the prom's color scheme. The atmosphere was pure joyful creativity. Not only did they learn baking techniques, they *owned* their learning at that moment. I saw introverted kids step into leadership and anxious kids relax into the flow of making. Neurodivergent learners often see patterns others miss, make innovative connections, and approach problems from unexpected angles. Joyful, creative environments not only make space for those strengths, but celebrate them as vital contributors to the learning community. When we intentionally design for joy and creativity, we communicate to every learner, "You belong here."

It's important to clarify: joy doesn't mean everything is easy or silly. Joy can come from deep absorption in work, from overcoming a challenge, from connecting with others. I've seen this time and time again as my students get lost in the art of cooking and baking. I love seeing their faces light up as they discover a flavor combination they've made is the perfect blend or when they present a beautifully plated dish. The *joy* of creating something personally meaningful unlocks the willingness to tackle the hard parts of the task. It echoes the story of Tommy the Dragon from our book, who found his voice through art when traditional learning failed him. Creativity was the key to revealing his brilliance. In our classrooms, when we allow students to bring their interests and imagination into the work, we often witness a similar unlocking of potential.

How can we practically infuse joy and creativity into CTE lessons? Sometimes it's by incorporating playful themes or narratives. For example, turning a cupcake unit into "Cupcake Wars" and having students create their own unique theme and flavor profile. Other times it's by giving students a real-world problem to solve that connects to their lives, like creating a noodle dish with a package of ramen and the leftover ingredients in the refrigerator. We can also celebrate creativity by showcasing student work by catering prom, a teacher appreciation lunch, or a senior carnival. The pride students feel when their work is appreciated is pure joy, and it reinforces the idea that their creative efforts matter.

Additionally, embracing student creativity can increase their sense of ownership and agency. When a learner sees their idea come to life whether it's a recipe, a fashion design, or a childcare game they invented, they internalize the lesson far more deeply than if they were following a script. They also learn from each other. I often step back during these creative projects and notice students naturally teaching peers: "How did you get that frosting so smooth?" or "Can you show me how you created that plating design?" The classroom becomes a collaborative space that allows students to bring out the best in each other.

Joy in learning is crucial, and so is joy in teaching. When you as the teacher are enjoying the process, students sense it. I let my own personality show in my teaching and come authentically as myself each and every day. I stand by my door to greet students daily with a smile and a hello, addressing each student by name. This simple and intentional act sets the tone for that class period. Students know I'm excited they are there and regardless of what happened the class period before. I also am not afraid to try a silly game idea that I just thought of or to introduce a challenge inspired by a new reality game show I watched the previous week.

This not only models vulnerability and passion, but it also makes the classroom a safe space for students to be themselves. They know they are welcome and free to be authentically themselves. Neurodivergent students, who may feel pressure to conform elsewhere, often *relax* when they see their teacher being authentically joyful and even a bit goofy. It gives them permission to drop the mask too. The Dragon Smart philosophy encourages us to be champions of our students' unique strengths; part of that is creating a classroom culture where joy and creativity are normalized. Students feel safe proposing an off-the-wall idea, and we say, "Let's give it a try!" rather than "No, that's not in the curriculum." Of course, we still meet our standards and learning goals, but we do it in a way that honors student voice and choice.

Imagine a CTE classroom that hums not with boredom or stress, but with the vibrant energy of students who are engrossed, playful, and creative. That vision is within reach when we teach with an inclusive heart and a joyful spirit. By bringing the Dragon Smart philosophy to life, seeing the brilliance in every learner, and lighting the fire of joy in our teaching we not only educate our students in skills and content, we also affirm their worth and potential. An inclusive, joyful CTE classroom doesn't just produce good projects; it helps grow confident, creative, and engaged young people who know their unique way of thinking is a gift. And that, to me, is the ultimate recipe for success.

CHAPTER 9

From Tears to Triumph

When Students Lead the Way

THE MAGIC LIVES ON

As we come to the final pages of this journey, I want to remind you of something powerful: The magic was never in a game, a strategy, a lesson plan, or a technology. It's in *you*, the educator brave enough to believe that school can be a place where students light up instead of shut down. The teacher who dares to take risks, play boldly, and reimagine what learning can look like. The one who sees potential in every student, even (and especially) the ones the system hasn't always seen clearly.

When I returned to the classroom after years away, I wondered if the magic I once knew had faded. I questioned whether students had changed too much, or whether I had. But the truth I've discovered over and over again is that while the world may have shifted, the essential needs of learners have not. They still crave connection. They still light up with curiosity. They still grow through challenge and joy. And when we intentionally design for those things, magic happens.

This book is a collection of those intentional designs, lessons woven with wonder, games that make learning stick, classrooms that include *every* learner, and stories that remind us why we chose this calling in the first place. We've explored how to:

- ✳ Take bold risks to bring joy and creativity into your teaching
- ✳ Use the MAGICAL Learning Experience Planning System to plan engaging and meaningful units and lessons
- ✳ Build trust and community from day one through challenges and connections
- ✳ Remix board games, reality TV shows, and creative tools into memorable learning adventures
- ✳ Harness curiosity through mystery, art, and play
- ✳ Use AI not to replace your creativity, but to expand it
- ✳ Support neurodivergent learners with practices that foster belonging, dignity, and joy

Each chapter was an invitation to look at learning through a new lens. But more importantly, it was a reminder that *you* are the greatest tool in your classroom. When you model curiosity, your students become curious. When you lead with playfulness, they begin to take risks. When you believe in their magic, they begin to believe in their own.

THE YEAR OF TEARS

Student and teacher belief in their own magic matters not only on good days. It matters on the awful ones too. Case in point: If someone had told me that the class I would cry in front of twice this year would end up being the class that taught me the most about connection, trust, and community, I'm not sure I would've believed them.

The first time I broke down was early in the year. I had returned to classroom teaching after what felt like a lifetime away, full of ideas and excitement. But this group? They were different. The personalities were strong. The energy was unpredictable. The learning styles were diverse and complex. I couldn't find the rhythm.

That day, an argument broke out mid-class. Students were openly questioning the way I was teaching. There was tension in the air that felt too heavy to carry. I held it together until the bell rang. It was then that I crumbled. The tears wouldn't stop streaming. I still vividly remember the thoughts that were running through my mind in that moment. *This is so hard. Maybe I'm not the right person for this. Maybe I've been away too long. Maybe I'm out of step with what students need.*

But the next day, I came back.

Not with all the answers. Not with a perfect plan. But I showed up and I kept showing up. I tweaked lessons, tried new strategies, laughed more, listened more, and celebrated even the smallest wins. I worked hard to build community, even when it didn't feel like it was working. I layered in challenges, games, opportunities for student voice. I tried to meet them where they were, even when I wasn't sure where that was.

For a long time, it felt like I was pouring into a classroom that wasn't pouring back.

Until it did.

THE SECOND CRY

Fast forward six months.

I knew I was hitting my limit when the second thing shattered.

It had already been one of those days. In the first block of the day, a plate shattered. In the second block, a glass broke so dramatically we were finding glass shards from across the kitchen. To make matters worse, I had miscalculated the time needed for a lab, and as a result, my students were frantically racing around the kitchen finishing cleanup and trying with all their might to get their cakes to bake faster. The bell rang and cakes were still in the oven, making students tardy for their next class.

I took a deep breath as my advanced class started trickling into the classroom chaos. Then, the final straw fell. One of my advanced students, who held the key knowledge of a recipe we were preparing for a catered event, came to tell me she wouldn't be in class due to an unexpected doctor's appointment.

I tried to pull it together by stepping out of the classroom for a moment. I thought I had been successful. I went back inside, welcomed the students, said, "it's been a day, and I'm stressed." That's when it happened.

Tears. Right there, in front of my advanced class.

I wanted to hold it together. I wanted to be a composed, calm leader. But the stress of catering back-to-back events, combined with the relentless undercurrent of anxiety that had been slowly mounting, cracked me open in the most vulnerable of ways.

And then something magical happened.

My students didn't flinch. They didn't laugh. They didn't look away. They rallied.

Without skipping a beat, they started moving. They each took ownership of a dish that still needed to be prepared for the luncheon and took charge to organize themselves and make it happen. The next day, when it all mattered the most, they came in early to help prepare for the event and stayed late to clean up after. I didn't ask them, they just did it. They stepped in, stepped up, and showed me what community really looks like.

It was messy. Unplanned. Raw. And absolutely beautiful.

WHEN I COULDN'T LEAD, THEY DID

That was the moment I realized: All of the messy, hard, uncertain efforts from earlier in the year had been worth it. Every single awkward conversation. Every challenge that felt like a flop. Every day I'd showed up unsure but still gave it my all . . . it had built something.

So when I couldn't lead that day, they did.

They rose not because I had perfected the lesson plan, but because I had created a space over time where *they mattered*. Where their voices counted. Where we were in it together.

That's when I knew. We had become a family.

So, what made the difference? I've been thinking a lot about that question.

What changed?

What turned a class that once felt impossible into a team that carried the day when I couldn't?

Was it time?

Was it consistency?

Was it the trust that slowly, invisibly builds when you keep coming back with hope in your eyes?

I think it was all of that, and something more.

I think it was the power of being real. Not perfect. Not polished. Just real.

When we are brave enough to be authentic in front of our students, not just in our teaching, but in our full, human presence, we create the conditions for belonging. We show them that emotions are okay. That mistakes are survivable. That connection matters more than control.

LET THE MESS BE MAGICAL

There's this belief that strong teaching means having all the answers, always having control, never letting them see you sweat.

But I believe the opposite.

Strong teaching means being real.

It means showing emotion and showing up anyway.

It means trusting your students enough to let go sometimes so they can step forward.

That's what happened in my classroom. Not overnight. Not easily. But beautifully.

That second cry wasn't a breakdown, it was a breakthrough.

It was a moment that proved everything I had hoped was possible.

A classroom where students lead. Where the community is real. Where authenticity lives.

Where *learning is magical*, not because it's perfect, but because it's real.

Teaching is not a performance. It's a relationship.

And relationships take time, truth, and trust.

It won't always be obvious that the culture you're building is working. Some days, it may feel like it's falling apart. But then, without warning, it clicks. A student speaks up. A group pulls together. A moment cracks open, and the magic rushes in.

Not because everything went right. But because you stayed and you cared. You kept showing up. You kept believing in the process. You kept creating spaces where students could grow, lead, and care. And in doing so, they showed you what they were capable of.

This is what makes teaching magical. Not the games or the tech or the perfectly planned lesson. But the journey. The messy, emotional, unpredictable, glorious journey of growing a classroom into a community, one imperfect day at a time.

WHERE DO WE GO FROM HERE?

Let this final chapter be a beginning.

Go back through the chapters. Choose one strategy, one game, or one section that sparked an idea and try it. You don't need to do it all. You just need to start. Small changes, done consistently and with heart, ripple outward. One joyful lesson. One inclusive activity. One spark of curiosity at a time.

As you continue your journey, I invite you to:

Keep learning. Education is evolving, and so are we. Stay curious. Read widely. Experiment boldly.

Keep connecting. With students. With colleagues. With the incredible community of educators who are making learning magical all around the world.

Keep playing. Never underestimate the power of joy. It's not fluff, it's fuel.

Keep believing. In your students. In your craft. In the magic that happens when we create spaces where every learner can shine.

THE FINAL WORD

Years from now, your students may forget the specific content of a unit. But they won't forget *how* they felt in your class. They'll remember the teacher who saw them. The classroom where they laughed, learned, and belonged. The place where learning felt like an adventure.

Let this be your legacy: not just to teach content, but to create experiences that transform. The world doesn't need perfect teachers. It needs passionate ones. Playful ones. Purposeful ones.

It needs *you*.

So go out there and make learning magical—one day, one student, and one joyful spark at a time. You hold the magic!

Acknowledgments

This book was born from a deep love of teaching CTE and the belief that classrooms can be places of joy, creativity, and connection. To my husband, daughter, and son—thank you for filling my life with laughter, encouragement, and endless heart. You are my greatest adventure and the magic that grounds me when the world moves too fast.

To my students, past and present—thank you for inspiring me daily with your curiosity, courage, and creativity. You remind me why I fell in love with teaching in the first place and why I continue to believe in the power of play and possibility.

To my colleagues, mentors, and friends in education—thank you for cheering me on, challenging me to grow, and believing in this work. Your passion for learning and your commitment to students fuel my own.

To the incredible Dave Burgess Consulting family—thank you for helping bring my ideas to life and for creating a space where educators can share their stories with the world. I'm endlessly grateful for your support, guidance, and belief in me.

And finally, to every educator who dares to teach with heart, imagination, and courage—this book is for you. May it remind you that your classroom is a place where magic happens every day.

About Tisha Richmond

Tisha Richmond is a high school culinary arts teacher, author, podcast host, and education specialist from Southern Oregon. With over twenty years of experience in Family and Consumer Sciences and a background as a tech integration specialist, she brings creativity, innovation, and heart to education.

Tisha is the author of *Make Learning MAGICAL*, co-author of *The EduProtocol Companion Guide*, and co-author of the children's book *Dragon Smart*, written with her son, Tommy. Each of these works celebrates curiosity, creativity, and the power of playful learning experiences that engage and empower both students and educators.

A recipient of Medford School District's Golden Pear Secondary Teacher Award and Henry Ford Innovation Nation Educator Award (first place), Tisha was also honored with the Oregon Family and Consumer Science Distinguished Service Award in 2025.

Passionate about infusing joy, play, and purpose into learning, Tisha inspires educators around the globe to reimagine what's possible in their classrooms through gamified and innovative strategies. An energetic and heartfelt speaker, she empowers audiences to transform their teaching, spark creativity, and make learning truly MAGICAL.

Tisha is available for keynote presentations, workshops, professional development sessions, and consulting on a wide range of educational topics. Visit tisharichmond.com or contact her at makelearningmagical@gmail.com for more information.

More from Dave Burgess Consulting, Inc.

Since 2012, DBCI has published books that inspire and equip educators to be their best. For more information on our titles or to purchase bulk orders for your school, district, or book study, visit DaveBurgessConsulting.com/DBCIbooks.

THE *LIKE A PIRATE*™ SERIES

Teach Like a PIRATE by Dave Burgess

Balance Like a PIRATE by Jessica Cabeen, Jessica Johnson, and Sarah Johnson

eXPlore Like a PIRATE by Michael Matera

Learn Like a PIRATE by Paul Solarz

Plan Like a PIRATE by Dawn M. Harris

Play Like a PIRATE by Quinn Rollins

Run Like a PIRATE by Adam Welcome

Tech Like a PIRATE by Matt Miller

THE *LEAD LIKE A PIRATE*™ SERIES

Lead Like a PIRATE by Shelley Burgess and Beth Houf

Lead Beyond Your Title by Nili Bartley

Lead with Appreciation by Amber Teamann and Melinda Miller

Lead with Collaboration by Allyson Apsey and Jessica Gomez

Lead with Culture by Jay Billy

Lead with Instructional Rounds by Vicki Wilson

Lead with Literacy by Mandy Ellis

She Leads by Dr. Rachael George and Majalise W. Tolan

THE EDUPROTOCOL FIELD GUIDE SERIES

Deploying EduProtocols by Kim Voge, with Jon Corippo and Marlena Hebern

The EduProtocol Field Guide by Marlena Hebern and Jon Corippo

The EduProtocol Field Guide Book 2 by Marlena Hebern and Jon Corippo

The EduProtocol Field Guide ELA Edition by Jacob Carr

The EduProtocol Field Guide Math Edition by Lisa Nowakowski and Jeremiah Ruesch

The EduProtocol Field Guide Primary Edition by Benjamin Cogswell and Jennifer Dean

The EduProtocol Field Guide Social Studies Edition by Dr. Scott M. Petri and Adam Moler

LEADERSHIP & SCHOOL CULTURE

Autopilot by Rich Czyz

Be 1% Better by Ron Clark

Be THAT Teacher by Dwayne Reed

Beyond the Surface of Restorative Practices by Marisol Rerucha

Change the Narrative by Henry J. Turner and Kathy Lopes

Choosing to See by Pamela Seda and Kyndall Brown

Culturize by Jimmy Casas

Discipline Win by Andy Jacks

Educate Me! by Dr. Shree Walker with Michael D. Ison

Escaping the School Leader's Dunk Tank by Rebecca Coda and Rick Jetter

Fight Song by Kim Bearden

From Teacher to Leader by Starr Sackstein

If the Dance Floor Is Empty, Change the Song by Joe Clark

The Innovator's Mindset by George Couros

It's OK to Say "They" by Christy Whittlesey

Kids Deserve It! by Todd Nesloney and Adam Welcome

Leading the Whole Teacher by Allyson Apsey

Let Them Speak by Rebecca Coda and Rick Jetter

The Limitless School by Abe Hege and Adam Dovico

Live Your Excellence by Jimmy Casas

Next-Level Teaching by Jonathan Alsheimer

The Pepper Effect by Sean Gaillard

Principaled by Kate Barker, Kourtney Ferrua, and Rachael George

The Principled Principal by Jeffrey Zoul and Anthony McConnell

Relentless by Hamish Brewer

The Secret Solution by Todd Whitaker, Sam Miller, and Ryan Donlan

Start. Right. Now. by Todd Whitaker, Jeffrey Zoul, and Jimmy Casas

Stop. Right. Now. by Jimmy Casas and Jeffrey Zoul

Teach Your Class Off by CJ Reynolds

Teachers Deserve It by Rae Hughart and Adam Welcome

They Call Me "Mr. De" by Frank DeAngelis

Thrive Through the Five by Jill M. Siler

Unmapped Potential by Julie Hasson and Missy Lennard

When Kids Lead by Todd Nesloney and Adam Dovico

Word Shift by Joy Kirr

Your School Rocks by Ryan McLane and Eric Lowe

TECHNOLOGY & TOOLS

50 Things to Go Further with Google Classroom by Alice Keeler and Libbi Miller

50 Things You Can Do with Google Classroom by Alice Keeler and Libbi Miller

50 Ways to Engage Students with Google Apps by Alice Keeler and Heather Lyon

140 Twitter Tips for Educators by Brad Currie, Billy Krakower, and Scott Rocco

AI Optimism by Becky Keene

Block Breaker by Brian Aspinall

Building Blocks for Tiny Techies by Jamila "Mia" Leonard

Code Breaker by Brian Aspinall

The Complete EdTech Coach by Katherine Goyette and Adam Juarez

Control Alt Achieve by Eric Curts

The Esports Education Playbook by Chris Aviles, Steve Isaacs, Christine Lion-Bailey, and Jesse Lubinsky

Google Apps for Littles by Christine Pinto and Alice Keeler

Master the Media by Julie Smith

Raising Digital Leaders by Jennifer Casa-Todd

Reality Bytes by Christine Lion-Bailey, Jesse Lubinsky, and Micah Shippee, PhD

Sail the 7 Cs with Microsoft Education by Becky Keene and Kathi Kersznowski

Shake Up Learning by Kasey Bell

Social LEADia by Jennifer Casa-Todd

Stepping Up to Google Classroom by Alice Keeler and Kimberly Mattina

Teaching Math with Google Apps by Alice Keeler and Diana Herrington

Teaching with Google Jamboard by Alice Keeler and Kimberly Mattina

Teachingland by Amanda Fox and Mary Ellen Weeks

TEACHING METHODS & MATERIALS

All 4s and 5s by Andrew Sharos

Boredom Busters by Katie Powell

Building Strong Writers by Christina Schneider

The Classroom Chef by John Stevens and Matt Vaudrey

The Collaborative Classroom by Trevor Muir

Copyrighteous by Diana Gill

CREATE by Bethany J. Petty

Ditch That Homework by Matt Miller and Alice Keeler

Ditch That Textbook by Matt Miller

Don't Ditch That Tech by Matt Miller, Nate Ridgway, and Angelia Ridgway

EDrenaline Rush by John Meehan

Educated by Design by Michael Cohen, The Tech Rabbi

Empowered to Choose: A Practical Guide to Personalized Learning by Andrew Easton

Expedition Science by Becky Schnekser

Frustration Busters by Katie Powell

Fully Engaged by Michael Matera and John Meehan

Game On? Brain On! by Lindsay Portnoy, PhD

Guided Math AMPED by Reagan Tunstall

Happy & Resilient by Roni Habib

Innovating Play by Jessica LaBar-Twomy and Christine Pinto

Instant Relevance by Denis Sheeran

Instructional Coaching Connection by Nathan Lang-Raad

Keeping the Wonder by Jenna Copper, Ashley Bible, Abby Gross, and Staci Lamb

LAUNCH by John Spencer and A.J. Juliani

Learning in the Zone by Dr. Sonny Magana

Less Talk, More Action by Allyson Apsey and Emily Freeland

Lights, Cameras, TEACH! by Kevin J. Butler

Make Learning MAGICAL by Tisha Richmond

Pass the Baton by Kathryn Finch and Theresa Hoover

Project-Based Learning Anywhere by Lori Elliott

Pure Genius by Don Wettrick

The Revolution by Darren Ellwein and Derek McCoy

The Science Box by Kim Adsit and Adam Peterson

Shift This! by Joy Kirr

Skyrocket Your Teacher Coaching by Michael Cary Sonbert

Spark Learning by Ramsey Musallam

Sparks in the Dark by Travis Crowder and Todd Nesloney

Table Talk Math by John Stevens

Teachables by Cheryl Abla and Lisa Maxfield

Unpack Your Impact by Naomi O'Brien and LaNesha Tabb

The Wild Card by Hope and Wade King

Writefully Empowered by Jacob Chastain

The Writing on the Classroom Wall by Steve Wyborney

You Are Poetry by Mike Johnston

You'll Never Guess What I'm Saying by Naomi O'Brien

You'll Never Guess What I'm Thinking About by Naomi O'Brien

INSPIRATION, PROFESSIONAL GROWTH & PERSONAL DEVELOPMENT

Be REAL by Tara Martin

Be the One for Kids by Ryan Sheehy

The Coach ADVenture by Amy Illingworth

Creatively Productive by Lisa Johnson

The Ed Branding Book by Dr. Renae Bryant and Lynette White

Educational Eye Exam by Alicia Ray

The EduNinja Mindset by Jennifer Burdis

Empower Our Girls by Lynmara Colón and Adam Welcome

Finding Lifelines by Andrew Grieve and Andrew Sharos

The Four O'Clock Faculty by Rich Czyz

How Much Water Do We Have? by Pete and Kris Nunweiler

P Is for Pirate by Dave and Shelley Burgess

A Passion for Kindness by Tamara Letter

The Path to Serendipity by Allyson Apsey

PheMOMenal Teacher by Annick Rauch

Recipes for Resilience by Robert A. Martinez

Rogue Leader by Rich Czyz

Sanctuaries by Dan Tricarico

Saving Sycamore by Molly B. Hudgens

The Secret Sauce by Rich Czyz

Shattering the Perfect Teacher Myth by Aaron Hogan

Stories from Webb by Todd Nesloney

Talk to Me by Kim Bearden

Teach Better by Chad Ostrowski, Tiffany Ott, Rae Hughart, and Jeff Gargas

Teach Me, Teacher by Jacob Chastain

Teach, Play, Learn! by Adam Peterson

The Teachers of Oz by Herbie Raad and Nathan Lang-Raad

Teaching Is a Tattoo by Mike Johnston

Teaching the Ms. Abbott Way by Joyce Stephens Abbott

TeamMakers by Laura Robb and Evan Robb

Through the Lens of Serendipity by Allyson Apsey

Write Here and Now by Dan Tricarico

The Zen Teacher by Dan Tricarico

CHILDREN'S BOOKS

The Adventures of Little Mickey by Mickey Smith Jr.

Alpert by LaNesha Tabb

Alpert & Friends by LaNesha Tabb

Beyond Us by Aaron Polansky

Cannonball In by Tara Martin

Dolphins in Trees by Aaron Polansky

Dragon Smart by Tisha and Tommy Richmond

I Can Achieve Anything by MoNique Waters

I Want to Be a Lot by Ashley Savage

The Magic of Wonder by Jenna Copper, Ashley Bible, Abby Gross, and Staci Lamb

Micah's Big Question by Naomi O'Brien

The Princes of Serendip by Allyson Apsey

Ride with Emilio by Richard Nares

A Teacher's Top Secret Confidential by LaNesha Tabb

A Teacher's Top Secret: Mission Accomplished by LaNesha Tabb

The Wild Card Kids by Hope and Wade King

Zom-Be a Design Thinker by Amanda Fox

www.ingramcontent.com/pod-product-compliance
Lightning Source LLC
Chambersburg PA
CBHW050527170426
43201CB00013B/2108